The Way of the Lord: Plotting St. Luke's Itinerary

The Way of the Lord: Plotting St. Luke's Itinerary

A Pedagogical Aid

Eugene E. Lemcio

WIPF & STOCK · Eugene, Oregon

THE WAY OF THE LORD: PLOTTING ST. LUKE'S ITINERARY
A Pedagogical Aid

Wipf & Stock
An Imprint of Wipf and Stock Publishers
199 W. 8th Ave., Suite 3
Eugene, OR 97401

www.wipfandstock.com

PAPERBACK ISBN: 978-1-7252-6232-4
HARDCOVER ISBN: 978-1-7252-6233-1
EBOOK ISBN: 978-1-7252-6234-8

Manufactured in the U.S.A. 03/16/20

Contents

Abbreviations

AAA	Adoption, Adaptation, Arrangement (= redaction)
AB	Anchor Bible
ANF	Ante-Nicene Fathers of the Christian Church
AV	Authorized Version
BAR	*Biblical Archaeology Review*
BCE	Before the Common Era
BR	*Biblical Research*
BTB	*Biblical Theology Bulletin*
C & D	Cartlidge, David R., and Dungan, David, eds. *Documents for the Study of the Gospels.* Minneapolis: Fortress, 1980.
CATR	*Canadian-American Theological Review*
CE	Common Era
CT	*Christianity Today*
DSS	Dead Sea Scrolls
ET	English Translation
FG	Fourth Gospel (= the Gospel According to St. John)
GNT	Greek New Testament
GOT	Greek Old Testament (= LXX)
HB	Hebrew Bible
IEJ	*Israel Exploration Journal*
JB	Jerusalem Bible
JBL	*Journal of Biblical Literature*
JSNT	*Journal for the Study of the New Testament*

JTS	*Journal of Theological Studies*
KJV	King James Version
L	Material found only in Luke
LCL	Loeb Classical Library
LXX	Septuagint of the Greek Old Testament (= OG)
M	Material found only in Matthew
ms.	Manuscript
mss.	Manuscripts
MT	Masoretic Text of the Hebrew Bible
NC	New Covenant
NEB	New English Bible
NETS	New English Translation of the Septuagint
NRSV	New Revised Standard Version
NT	New Testament
NTS	*New Testament Studies*
OC	Old Covenant
OG	Old Greek (= LXX)
OGI	*Orientis Graeci Inscriptiones Selectae*
OSB	Orthodox Study Bible
OT	Old Testament
Q	Material, whether oral or written, found primarily in Matthew & Luke
RSV	Revised Standard Version
SBLDS	Society of Biblical Literature Dissertation Series
SG	Synoptic Gospel(s)
SNTSMS	Society for New Testament Studies Monograph Series
TB	*Tyndale Bulletin*
TT	Triple Tradition (material shared by all three SG)

Definitions

AAA	"Adopt," "Adapt," "Arrange." My own acronym for the essential operations of what is called "Redaction Criticism" (or "History of Redaction" = *Redaktionsgeschichte*), by which an Evangelist chose, modified, and positioned his received traditions (either oral or written). Studying the result or the last stage of redaction criticism is sometimes called "composition criticism."
Apocrypha	Lit. "hidden" (either because special or suspect—depending on the user). Protestant usage (following Jerome) is exclusively pejorative. Roman Catholic and Eastern churches apply it to different writings.
Comparison	Relations between like or similar subjects
Contrast	Relations between diverse subjects
Deuterocanon	Lit. "second canon"—a term devised in the sixteenth century and used as a less pejorative, more neutral term than "apocrypha" to distinguish documents originally composed (it was then thought[1]) in Greek and therefore not (as) authoritative as the "protocanonicals." These sixty-six books correspond to the

1. Since 1948, several have been found among the Dead Sea Scrolls written in Hebrew or Aramaic.

	Hebrew canon finally delimited by Jews during the early centuries CE.
Disciple	Both the Greek and Latin words that this translates are the normal terms for student/learner. Other languages convey such a sense more directly.
Gentile	From the Latin *gentes* ("nations"); i.e., all the nations besides Israel, non-Jews
L	Material found in Luke alone (a source: oral, written?)
Logos	Greek for "Word" or "Message"
M	Material found in Matthew alone (a source: oral, written?)
Myth(s)	Foundational narrative(s)—rich in symbol and metaphor—about the origins, meaning, and destiny of the cosmos and human existence. Its imagery is primordial with regard to origins, eschatological in consequence, and contemporaneous in significance.[2]
Mythaphor[3]	Metaphor found in mythic narrative
Of	In Greek, as in English, this word (grammatically, a genitive) can suggest possession ("this book of mine" or "*my* book"), origination ("Jesus *from* Nazareth"), objectivity ("the Gospel *about* Jesus"), and subjectivity ("the Gospel *by* Jesus").
Prophet	From the Greek, meaning "to speak on behalf of." Sometimes, the distinction is made between "forth-telling" and "foretelling." Classical prophets such as Elijah and Elisha did little, if any, predicting of the future.
Protocanon	See "Deuterocanon," above.
Pseudepigrapha	Lit. "false ascription," a derogatory, artificial term applied to literature regarded as falsely attributed to an

2. Zaleski, *Fellowship*, 4: "the regenerative power of story."

3. I take full responsibility for this neologism.

	ancient worthy. Those by whom the texts were preserved obviously thought otherwise.
Q	From the German *Quelle* (= "source"), thought to be a source (oral? written?) adopted, adapted, and arranged by Matthew and Luke. I use it as a convenient means of referring to material found in both Evangelists.
Redaction Criticism	See AAA, above.
Synoptic	A "seeing together," the term being applied to the first three Gospels, whose authors, despite their differences, are distinct from the Gospel of John in content and manner of presentation.
Triple Tradition	Material that all three Synoptic Evangelists contain in varying degrees

Preface

> The truth is, when all is said and done, one does not teach a subject, one teaches a student how to learn it.[1]

THIS IS THE FOURTH volume in an informal series of works[2] that aim to assist both teacher and student in preparation for instruction and learning, both within and beyond the college or seminary classroom. Before expounding my approach further, a word needs to be said about the title. I have again attempted to approximate in it the cadence of the previous three while trying also to indicate the connection between title and subject matter. Although each of the Gospels presents the ministry of John the Baptizer against the backdrop of Isaiah 40, it is Luke who quotes the passage at greatest length. Hence, "The Way of the Lord," so prominent in that text, seemed appropriate.[3]

If one also takes into account the Evangelist's extensive "Travel Narrative" 9:51—19:27), then the journey that the Lord (Jesus) takes to Jerusalem continues to sustain this motif.[4] However, "way" can mean not only direction or itinerary but also character or manner—as in "The way we were" or "She has a certain way about her." Finally, although more playful than anything else, I have chosen "plotting" for a secondary reason: to rhyme with "plodding"—in keeping with the traditional, ecclesiastical symbol associating the Third Gospel with an ox (one of several, different sacrificial

1. Barzun, "Reasons to De-Test the Schools."

2. Lemcio, *Navigating*; *Travels*; *Soaring*.

3. In the book of Acts, Jesus' disciples belong to or are followers of "The Way [of the Lord]": 9:2; 13:10; 18:26; 19:9, 23; 22:4; 24:14, 22.

4. Forward, "Pilgrimage of Grace," also identifies mini-journeys taken by both Jesus and by various characters in the narrative.

animals[5]), an image that Richard Burridge[6] has expounded as characteristic of the deliberate, steady pace by which Jesus moves from womb to tomb, from manger to Emmaus—via Calvary. But we must ever keep in mind that it is Luke himself who plots this journey.[7]

Disclaimers

This is not a historical quest aimed at reconstructing the traditions (oral or written) or identifying the sources (oral or written) that Luke used to compose his Gospel. Such study runs the risk of becoming a history of early Christian religion—a legitimate scholarly pursuit in its own right. My work stands somewhere between an exercise in redaction criticism (whereby one studies how the Evangelist adopted (chose), adapted (modified), and arranged (organized) his materials about Jesus and an exercise in literary criticism, which focuses upon the development of characters and plots. I am inclined to regard that which follows as an attempt at what might be called "composition criticism."[8]

Furthermore, the comparisons and contrasts that I make between Luke and the other Gospels do not rest upon a rigid theory of Gospel relationships. When I refer to Q, it is simply shorthand for material common

5. The blood of oxen ritualized the bond between God and Israel (Exod 24:1–8); the blood of lambs provided protection from the Angel of Death striking first-born sons throughout Egypt (Exodus 12). However, on the Day of Atonement, a *live* goat bore the People's sins from the encampment into the desert (Leviticus 19). I mention these now in anticipation of later discussion about Luke's "atonement theology," which Hans Conzelmann (in)famously declared the Third Evangelist did not possess: *Theology of St. Luke*, 200–201. Such pronouncements run the risk of betraying a kind of preferential paulinism or confessionalism that should have no bearing upon attempts to exegete the mind of this Gospel composer.

6. Burridge, *Four Gospels*, 98–129. I have always found it curious that, in the history of Christian symbolism, Luke's Gospel has been portrayed as an ox whereas Matthew's Gospel has been rendered with a human face. Surely, the Jesus of the Third Gospel is no less human than his Matthean counterpart. And the Jesus of the First Gospel (1:23, 26:28) is no less a sacrificial figure than he is in Luke.

7. I have consequently referred to the chapter divisions in this book as "Plots."

8. Those who look to my work for evidence by which to reconstruct the so-called "historical Jesus" or for data regarding the church for whom the author of the Third Gospel wrote will be disappointed. Each of these endeavors can be a legitimate academic exercise in its own right. However, both must (1) begin with the hardest data available (the text bequeathed by the early church) and then (2) work backwards towards their origin(s) so as to reduce, if not avoid, circularity.

to both Matthew and Luke. Whether or not it was an oral or written source plays no part in my attempts to get at Luke's distinctive message(s). Fortunately, debates about Gospel priorities need not be engaged in this instance. Luke will have followed either Mark or Matthew.[9] Examining how Luke differs from the others is a clue to significance, especially if such differentiation is frequent and consistent in content. "L" simply stands for material found only in Luke. Regularity of content in such instances also suggests the hues that Luke used to paint the portrait of his Subject.

This is not a commentary whereby one is obliged to cover just about everything. Although at least some part of nearly every chapter is touched upon, I have not tried to be complete. Rather, my aim has been to highlight that which is characteristic of the Gospel—that which makes Luke Luke. It ought not to be thought of as a stand-alone work. Rather, it should be used alongside other, more standard resources: commentaries, introductions, lexical helps,[10] "background" studies about Second Temple Judaism and the Greco-Roman world, etc.

Affirmations

My book, like the other three, is meant to encourage and enhance first-hand engagement with the text—employing both sides of the brain (hemisphericity) visualizing and verbalizing, displaying as well as discussing, seeing as well as saying, showing as well as telling. Such is my distinctive contribution. Not everything is covered in this dual manner, partly because not everything lends itself to both types of presentation. One desired outcome of providing such materials and methods is to promote discovery, exploration, and one's own investigation. As a further "aid" to this educational enterprise (new to this volume) is the explicit statement of goals for each exercise.

Another strategy to foster such learning is the posing of questions, familiar to police interrogations and to students of journalism needing to cover all of a story's or a statement's bases: Who? (Agent: initiator or recipient), What? (Action/Event), When? (Time), Where? (Place), How? (Means/Manner/Method/Instrument), How Far/Many/Much? (Scope/Quantity), What Kind? (Quality), Why? (Purpose/Cause), So What? (Significance),

9. Arguments that Matthew used Luke are not compelling, in my view. Too many qualifications are required.

10. Although I have not presupposed knowledge of Hebrew; Aramaic; Greek; and Latin, I occasionally cite biblical languages where they help to illuminate the text further.

etc.[11] Once again, not all the material lends itself to this mode of analysis and presentation; the kind of genre plays a part.

Using these categories enables analysis and synthesis to be *comprehensive* in the sense that many aspects of a selected narrative or teaching can be dealt with. At the same time, they make it possible for one to detect that which *integrates* the parts. Approaching literature in this way assists students to develop skills in *comparison* (noting similarities) and *contrast* (seeing differences). Furthermore, applying such neutral classification helps to *increase objectivity* and to limit imposing agendas foreign to a text.

No rigid sequence needs to be followed when employing the above. They can be freely re-ordered to achieve the greatest pedagogical effect. However, it is generally good practice to get an idea of the entire context, to see the forest within which individual trees grow, and to survey the lay of the land. Besides providing a sense of the whole, from which to interpret the parts, the bird's eye view enables one to get a feel for proportion—where the emphases lie, what weight is attributed to certain themes.

In addition to leading the reader in comparing and contrasting categories within the text itself (thereby allowing the Evangelist to speak on his own terms and in his own way—the main objective), I provide opportunities for readers to compare and contrast the Gospel with external sources—both canonical and extra-biblical. Examples of the former are of two kinds: (a) the OT Scriptures acknowledged by all Christians and (b) the New Testament. "Extra-biblical" sources refers to Jewish literature such as the Dead Sea Scrolls (DSS) and to Greco-Roman texts. This is an attempt to provide for modern readers samples of the literary environment that shaped the religious world of Jesus, Luke, and the earliest Christians. They enable one to visualize the similarities and differences (the continuity and discontinuity) between "Athens and Jerusalem."

So far as the remainder of the NT is concerned, I have studiously avoided interpreting Luke with reference to other authors. However, in the case of the SG, some accounts of the same event or teaching are similar enough that the Plots will do double and even triple duty in providing a procedure by which one can subsequently study the others on their own.[12] Rather than diluting the work and taking away from its distinctiveness by

11. Many of these categories and procedures are enshrined in Traina, *Methodical Bible Study*.

12. My next effort is titled, *The King Who Teaches: St. Matthew's Royal Curriculum. A Pedagogical Aid.*

harmonizing, such a move serves to highlight the salient features of Luke by maintaining the integrity of the others.

Once again, I have used the NRSV, except in those passages referring to the son of man (where I resort to the RSV). I did so principally because this translation has preserved the expression rather than converting it to the generic "human" or "mortal." Although not a title *per se*, the term retains a certain formal quality, which NT writers exploit when they appropriate it. Such usage is obscured by the NRSV's otherwise welcome efforts to avoid gender specific translation.

When all of this is said and done, it is the instructor of a particular class who bears the responsibility of using these tools and other techniques to engage in the complex act of pedagogy. Ink on a page cannot teach; nor can literature fulfill literature. The Bible *per se* is unable to do so. Although notable exceptions might be cited, one needs the help of an agent—as the encounter between Philip and Ethiopian eunuch shows (Acts 8:30–35). The identity of the Servant in Isaiah 53 was not self-evident. According to Luke's first volume, it had taken a special act of the risen Jesus to open the eyes of the disciples to see in the Scriptures that the Messiah had to suffer (Luke 24:44–46).[13]

While it is true that none of my books advocating these approaches has been systematic and thoroughgoing (as required in a commentary), they have attempted to be orderly and disciplined. Nevertheless, teachers should be free from the burden of using all of the plots within a quarter or semester setting. Nor should one be obliged to follow the same sequence. Furthermore, if instructor or student asks, "Why was this passage or that subject not covered by the author?" the response should be, "Well, given the tools and method provided, let's try filling in the gaps!"

Although this is primarily a teaching/learning aid often reflecting common observations by Lukan specialists, I have also included unrefined bits of original research. In each of them, I have hinted at lines of inquiry that I (or others) might pursue. Although my aim has not been to propose a fresh thesis, I have in all four books made observations and raised questions that could bear additional fruit.

For those who will have experienced the Gospels' diversity for the first time (and perhaps been troubled by it), I supply in Appendix 1 a statement

13. Even an individual's encounter with a Gideon Bible, alone in a motel room, is dependent on someone's putting it there—and, beforehand, another's conveying the Semitic and Greek texts into the receiving language.

about such variety by Origen, the greatest biblical scholar of his era (the third century CE). This father of the church might have been wrong in these and other opinions; but what he held was considered within the bounds of that which a Christian was permitted to think. Such knowledge might possibly reduce (if not remove) some of the unnecessary heat often generated in contemporary debates about the Bible's nature.

Perhaps the most controversial sections of this study for more conservative readers will be the "parallels" that I have adduced between the Gospel story and those about heroes in the ancient world:[14] miraculous conception, dual parentage (human mother, divine father, adoptive father), genealogical heritage, exalted names/titles, threatened childhood, mighty deeds/teaching, opposition, violent death, afterlife. Several reasons compel me to include them: (1) The common patterns exist; they cannot be denied. (2) Early Christian apologists critically engaged in debates about the similarities and differences of their content and morality.[15] (3) Until recent times, students receiving a classical education (both secular and ecclesial) would have encountered the stories. (4) Analogous accounts are being reintroduced into popular culture through books,[16] film,[17] and video games.[18] (5) Award-winning books/titles of children's literature[19] are readily available.

Although many have observed that Luke—presumably (though not definitely) a Gentile convert—nevertheless went to great lengths to root Christianity in the narratives and texts of God's original people, at the same

14. Of course, one needs to be careful about committing what Samuel Sandmel in an eponymous article famously termed "parallelomania." He described it as "that extravagance among scholars which first overdoes the supposed similarity in passages and then proceeds to describe source and derivation as if implying literary connection flowing in an inevitable or predetermined direction" (Sandmel, "Parallelomania," 1).

15. In Acts 17:18–29, Paul is reported as citing the truthful convictions of pagan poets regarding God and humanity's relation to the divine (vv. 18–19) since the philosophers on Mars Hill in Athens would not have regarded the Jewish Scriptures (even if known) as authoritative. Justin Martyr (second c. CE) engaged his contemporaries by comparing and contrasting Jesus with heroes of Greco-Roman myth: *Apology*, 1.21–23. See also van Kooten, "Christianity in the Graeco-Roman World."

16. From a Christian perspective, the works of C. S. Lewis come to mind, especially in the figure of Aslan in *The Lion, the Witch and the Wardrobe*. See also the discussion below in Plot 41, "Savior Gods," #3.

17. Several of Lewis's Chronicles of Narnia have been filmed.

18. Greek Gods Paradise, "88 Video Games Based on Greek Mythology."

19. Among them are D'Aulaire and D'Aulaire, *Book of Greek Myths*; Lipson et al., *Mighty Myth*; McCaughrean, *Hercules*; McDermott, *Arrow to the Sun* (Caldecott Medal Award winner for illustrating a Navajo myth).

time, he told the story (put his readers "in the frame") according to the well-known conventions of Greco-Roman biography with which Greek-speaking (that is, Hellenized) Jews would have been familiar.[20] As a basic pedagogical move, one might begin with Plot 42 to observe the overall narrative scheme of the Gospel in connection with such stories. This gives one a sense of the whole, a bird's eye view, the lay of the land, and the forest for the trees.

In this connection, some Evangelical readers will be surprised (and not a few troubled) that I freely use the word "myth" in a positive sense when relating Luke's Gospel to these accounts.[21] But I do so according to the understanding of the term employed by such classical scholars and convinced Christians as C. S. Lewis,[22] J. R. R. Tolkien,[23] and others.[24] Finally, all along the way, I have been supremely aware that one has to go "beyond the sacred page": that a menu is no substitute for a meal, nor is an itinerary (however sacred) a substitute for the journey.[25] In other words, the Third Gospel must, at the end of the day (and at its beginning?), be regarded as a religious document intended to form the reader's thinking and action as she/he relates to Jesus in community and the Way that he established.

20. I have made it a point to cite (among others) a complete, explicit example (that of Herakles)—not one requiring some assembly from various fragmentary sources—and one early enough not to have been itself influenced by Matthew and Luke. See "Savior Gods" in Plot 41.

21. A helpful treatment of the term's various uses can be conveniently accessed in Caird, *Language and Imagery*, 219–42. Still provocative is Barfield, "Meaning and Myth," 77–92. For a recent literary, historical, and theological treatment of the issue in general (and of Luke in particular), see Lincoln, *Born of a Virgin?*, 57–67 and 108–24.

22. Lewis, "Myth Became Fact," 63–67.

23. Fuller et al., *Myth, Allegory, and Gospel.*

24. See also Lockerbie, "Myth and Christian Reality"; Howard, "Myth: A Flight to Reality"; and Markos, "Myth Matters."

25. The first stanza of the Evangelical hymn "Break Thou the Bread of Life" contains the line, "beyond the sacred page, I seek Thee, Lord."

1

Luke 1:1–4.[1] Luke, the "Historian" (1 of 2)

Goal

Without joining the debate about the extent to which Luke might legitimately be regarded as a historian, we can (by comparing and contrasting him with the other Evangelists) at least attempt to assess his stated effort. In this connection, see the companion Plot 5 displaying and discussing his actual practice at 3:1–2. Ultimately, one needs to answer the all-important "So what?" question—that of significance. What was the point of his opening attempt at authorization, accreditation, access to sources, and use of certain methods?

1. The four passages following are from the RSV.

LUKE 1:1–4. LUKE, THE "HISTORIAN" (1 OF 2)

Matthew 1:1	Mark 1:1	Luke 1:1–4	John 20:30–31
"The book of the genealogy of Jesus Christ, the son of David, the son of Abraham."	"The beginning of the gospel of Jesus Christ, the Son of God."	"In as much as many have undertaken to compile a narrative of the things which have been accomplished among us, just as they were delivered to us by those who from the beginning were eyewitnesses and ministers of the word, it seemed good to me also, having followed closely for some time past, to write an orderly account for you, most excellent Theophilus, so that you may know the truth concerning the things of which you have been informed."	"Now Jesus did many other signs in the presence of his disciples, which are not written in this book; but these are written that you may believe that Jesus is the Christ, the Son of God, and that believing you may have life in his name." 21:24–25 "This is the disciple [cf. v. 23] who is bearing witness to these things, and who has written these things; and we know that his testimony is true. But there are also many other things which Jesus did; were every one of them to be written, I suppose that the world itself could not contain the books that would be written."

1. Matthew's opening lines alert the reader that the entire narrative is to be related to the genealogy that follows. Despite the fact that the First Evangelist regards Jesus to be God's Son, it is his descent ("sonship") from these two human ancestors that frames the account.
2. Mark's reference to "the beginning of the gospel" is debated. Does he mean events or persons in the subsequent verses; or is the entire narrative to be regarded as the gospel's beginning? For a review of ten different options, see Cranfield, *The Gospel According to Saint Mark*, 34–35. The Greek "of Jesus Christ," if an objective genitive, could mean "about Jesus Christ." If a subjective genitive, the gospel could be that which was proclaimed "by Jesus Christ."
3. Only the author/editor of the canonical FG identifies himself as an eyewitness, whose testimony is certified by an unknown collective: "we" (20:24). Furthermore, it is he who expresses his purpose

for writing in terms of believing in Jesus.[2] He admits to having been forced to be selective (v. 25).

4. Luke acknowledges the availability of other narratives (whether other Gospels or sources unknown to us) and signals his dependence on eyewitnesses, himself not being one. Rather, the Third Evangelist presents himself as an investigator. However, the sequence of events need not be limited to chronological order. It could be thematic or rhetorical (the one most likely to persuade).
5. The practice of history as a modern academic discipline involves the testing of sources' reliability. Does not even eyewitness testimony need to be cross-examined?[3] We do not know how much Luke engaged in this kind of activity. For a recent attempt to evaluate it, see Bauckham, *Jesus and the Eyewitnesses*, 116–24, and his reviewers.
6. Luke's purpose is catechetical: the schooling of Theophilus (whether an individual or a stand-in for all "lovers of God"). But that instruction is set within a context of people in charge (rulers temporal and spiritual) and within international, regional, and local settings—as Plot 5 for Luke 3:1–2 seeks to demonstrate.[4]

2. Manuscript evidence is divided over two readings, distinguished by a single letter (σ): one suggesting that non-Christian readers should "come to believe" (the inceptive or ingressive aorist), the other that Christians ought to "go on believing" (the continuous action of the so-called "present" tense). For a thorough discussion, see Metzger, *Textual Commentary*, 256.

3. The practice of historical investigation has been likened to that of judicial investigation—after both attorneys have vetted jury members (of the plaintiff's peers) for their impartiality. See especially Harvey's *The Historian and the Believer*.

4. For an important treatment of biography, historiography, and narratology, see Green, *Gospel of Luke*, 1–25.

2

Luke 1–2 & Matthew 1–2. Infancy Narratives in M & L[1]

Goal

Both in the church and in popular culture, the accounts of Matthew and Luke are nearly always conflated. However, doing so not only denies what the texts themselves actually say or do not say, it also obscures the special emphases that each Evangelist makes. Furthermore, such harmonizing prevents one from recognizing how the unique features of these introductory chapters set the stage for the narratives that follow: their orientation and subject matter. This Plot seeks to do justice to the diversity.

	Matthew 1–2 (M)	**Luke 1–2 (L)**
1. Headline	Book about Genealogy	Ordered Narrative
2. Christology (1)	Son of David & Abraham	-0-
3. Genealogy		
a. placement	Immediate	Between baptism & testing
b. sequence	Forwards from Abraham	Backwards from Jesus to Adam
c. pattern	3 sets of 14 generations	None obvious
d. content	Notorious, Gentile women	"Gentiles" fr. Abraham to Adam

1. Although his study concentrates on the Birth Narratives, much of what Andrew Lincoln (*Born of a Virgin?*) says about "parallels" with the genre of Greco-Roman biography could also apply to the fuller pattern with which I will subsequently deal at the end of the book (Plot 41). Of particular importance is his response to those who would insist that no monotheistic Jew would ever adopt or even adapt pagan patterns. While one can speak about the genus "Common Judaism" (Sanders, *Paul and Palestinian Judaism*), there existed many species of "Judaism" (Boyarin, *Jewish Gospels*)—among them being various expressions of Hellenistic Judaism, its members in touch with and appreciative of certain aspects of the wider Greco-Roman culture.

	Matthew 1–2 (M)	Luke 1–2 (L)
	Royal, reigning sons	Royal, not reigning sons (priests?)
4. Annunciation (1)	–0–	of John the Baptizer's birth a. to Zechariah [& Elizabeth] —1. both of priestly stock —2. both elderly —3. Elizabeth sterile b. by Angel Gabriel c. Zechariah's prophecy
5. Annunciation (2)	of Jesus' Birth a. to Joseph, son of David b. by Angel of the Lord c. to magi, by star	of Jesus' Birth a. to Mary, cousin of Elizabeth b. by Angel Gabriel c. her response: "Magnificat"[2] d. to shepherds, by angels
6. Christology (2)	Son, Immanuel, Christ Save the people from sins	Son of the Most High, Savior, Christ the Lord
7. Place (1)	Palace of Herod	Fields
8. Time	2 years later?	Soon after
9. Place (2)	House	Manger
10. Place (3)	–0–	Temple: circumcision, Passover
11. Place (4)	Egypt: flight & residence	–0–
12. Others	Magi a. Their persistence b. Their gifts	Anna, Simeon a. Her prophecy b. His "Nunc Dimittis"
13. Demography		
a. status	Upper echelons: pol & relig	Lower echelons
b. ethnicity	4 Gentile women & "magi"	More Gentiles in genealogy
14. Residence	Bethlehem, Egypt, Nazareth	Nazareth

1. Given the divergences between the two accounts, it is better to identify the "sources" as M and L rather than Q.

2. See the separate treatment of this passage in connection with "Hannah's Song" and Jesus' Beatitudes (Plot 4).

2. Although the focus here is on Luke, his distinctive contributions are made more vivid when compared and contrasted with Matthew's version.

3. Is it not odd that in Luke (at the very outset), there is no comparable high-powered Christology (of the kind found later in these chapters and throughout both Gospels)?

4. The Third Evangelist's list (l. 3c) is longer by an additional 47 ancestors. Matthew's totals 40 rather than 42, since David and Jeconiah are named at the end of one set and at the beginning of another.

5. No female ancestors appear in Luke's genealogy; but several older contemporaries of Jesus have significant roles in these opening chapters and throughout his Gospel: Elizabeth, Mary (ch. 1), the prophet Anna (2:36–38), highly placed, supportive followers (8:1–3), Mary and Martha (10:25–37).

6. Might the fact that none of the named *royal* sons in Luke actually *reigned* (unlike those in Matthew's list) be anticipated in the announcement made by Gabriel to Mary that Jesus was to occupy the throne of his ancestor, David, in an unconventional manner (1:32)?

7. Whose birth is narrated first? Is it significant that John the Baptizer should be accorded such priority and attention, as evidenced by the quantity of text and its placement? See Acts 19 (in Luke's Second Volume) for this desert preacher's far-flung influence: disciples in Ephesus, the second city of the Empire (having the political and commercial clout of New York City).

8. Would I be a Scrooge to point out that shepherds and magi were not at the manger at the same time? The latter visited the Holy Family in a house. And Herod's rampage (the "Slaughter of the Innocents") targeted children aged two years and under.

9. Read the offerings given by the Holy Parents in the light of Lev 12:8. How does this contribute to our knowledge of the family's (and Jesus') economic status?

10. The temple's setting and its *dramatis personae* (see also the opening chapters of Acts) testify to the significance of Christianity's roots in Judaism. If Luke was indeed a Gentile writing for a largely Gentile audience, then this point is doubly important.

3

Luke 1:37. "For nothing will be impossible with God."

Goal

To understand the Lukan birth narratives in connection with earlier biblical accounts of conceptions occurring contrary to the normal course of events and where women are at the center of attention[1] *(or are at least mentioned alongside men).*[2] *This is also one of several places where it is important to avoid two extremes: claiming too much or too little about similarities and differences.*

	Gen 18:1–15	1 Sam 1:1–20	Luke 1:5–25	Luke 1:26—2:7
1. Husband	Abraham	Elkanah	Zechariah	Joseph
2. Wife	Sarah	Hannah	Elizabeth	Mary
3. Obstacle	Age & Sterility	Sterility	Age & Sterility	Virginity
4. Divine agent	3 men/the Lord	the Lord	Angel of the Lord	Gabriel
5. Child	Isaac	Samuel	John	Jesus

1. Gabriel's words in Luke 1:37 echo those of Gen 18:14 and call to mind yet another birth occurring contrary to the normal course of physical events: 1 Sam 1:19–20.

1. The prophet Anna might be included in this regard, she being the only personage in the Third Gospel (besides John the Baptizer and Jesus) to be identified as such (2:36–38).

2. Such pairing occurs in the cases of Elizabeth and Zechariah, Mary and Joseph, and Anna and Simeon.

LUKE 1:37. "FOR NOTHING WILL BE IMPOSSIBLE WITH GOD."

2. Each of these, in its own way, involves divine intervention/creativity in an "impossible" situation: where biological facts preclude certain outcomes.
3. That is why some theologians see here a special creative act via divine agency: creation theology rather than atypical physiology, examples of which might be found throughout nature.

4

Luke 1:52–53. The Great Reversal

Hannah's Prayer, Mary's Magnificat,
Jesus' Beatitudes & Woes

Goal

It is often thought that revelation comes immediately from the divine to the human, especially in the case of Jesus: directly from Father to Son. However, the texts below testify to a more organic, mediated means. In this case, Jesus' teaching about God's reversing the fortunes of the power brokers and the powerless, the rich and the poor (especially prominent in Luke via L), has a prior history, both within the Third Gospel and within the full biblical canon. It is the purpose of this Plot to display and to reflect upon such relationships.

Hannah's Prayer (1 Sam 2:4–8)	Mary's Magnificat (1:52–53)	Jesus' Beatitudes & Woes (6:20–25)
1. "[God] raises the poor from the dust		"Blessed are you who are poor
2. [God] lifts the needy from the ash heap,	and lifted up the lowly."	
3. to make them sit with princes,	"He has brought down the powerful	
4. and inherit a seat of honor"	from their thrones,	for yours is the kingdom of God."
5. "The bows of the mighty are broken,		
but the feeble gird on strength."		

Hannah's Prayer (1 Sam 2:4–8)	**Mary's Magnificat (1:52–53)**	**Jesus' Beatitudes & Woes (6:20–25)**
6. "but those who were hungry	"He has filled the hungry	"Blessed are you who are hungry now,
7. are fat with spoil."	with good things	for you will be filled."
8.	and sent the rich away empty."	"But woe to you who are rich
9.		for you have received your consolation."
10. "Those who were full		"Woe to you who are full now
11. have hired themselves out for bread."		for you will be hungry."

1. Both political and economic issues are prominent in all three.
2. Luke is the one who directly addresses the poor and wealthy, the hungry and filled in the second person plural. And the Third Evangelist makes the point of having women voice these political and economic reversals.
3. Just as Mary drew on Hannah, so Jesus draws on the "songs" of both women—learned with his mother's milk and on her knees?
4. One can only wonder what heads of state and captains of industry have thought as they have heard/sung Mary's Magnificat in the liturgy during the two millennia since its composition. Or was their perception blocked by the filters of wealth, power, and status?
5. Note Fitzmyer, *Luke*, 360–61 on the aorist aspects of the verbs: are they the prophetic perfect of Hebrew expressions (conveyed idiomatically in Greek) or gnomic: the way that God typically works? Yet another grammatical possibility (the most likely, given the context) is the ingressive or inceptive aorist: the beginning/entry point of a condition or process. So, Mary's statements could begin with "God has begun to . . . ."
6. If tradition is correct that the James who wrote the eponymous Letter was the brother of Jesus, then the appearance of similar "family values" regarding rich and poor should not be surprising (2:1–7. Cf. 1:27).

5

Luke 3:1–2. Luke, the "Historian" (2 of 2)

Goal

To display the extensive way by which Luke has adopted L and OT material for his redactional purposes in relation to the other Gospels. What might attention to such details regarding personnel, their status, and geographical locations have accomplished for ancient readers? What might it do for today's faithful community?

Matthew 3:3	Mark 1:2–3	Luke 3:1–2	John 1:23
		"In the fifteenth year of the reign of Emperor Tiberius, when Pontius Pilate was governor of Judea, and Herod was ruler[1] of Galilee, and his brother Philip ruler of the region of Ituraea and Trachonitis, and Lysanias ruler of Abilene, during the high priesthood of Annas and Caiaphas, the word of God came to John son of Zechariah in the wilderness."	
		(vv. 4–6)	
Isaiah the prophet	Isaiah the prophet	the prophet Isaiah	Isaiah the prophet

1. The Greek word partially transliterated *tetrarch* originally referred to one ruling over a fourth of a region. Later it came to mean a dependent prince.

Matthew 3:3	Mark 1:2–3	Luke 3:1–2	John 1:23
"The voice of one crying in the wilderness:"	"The voice of one crying in the wilderness:"	"The voice of one crying in the wilderness:"	"the voice of one crying out in the wilderness,"
"Prepare the way of the Lord,"	"Prepare the way of the Lord,"	"Prepare the way of the Lord,"	"the way of the Lord"
"make his paths straight."	"make his paths straight."	"make his paths straight."	"Make straight . . . ."
		"Every valley shall be filled, and every mountain and hill shall be made low, and the crooked shall be made straight, and the rough ways shall be made smooth; and all flesh shall see the salvation of God."	

1. We do not have to join the debate about the historical trustworthiness of Luke's Gospel (and Acts) to acknowledge the Evangelist's desire to locate his narrative (1:1) within the context of international, national, regional, and local history. This effort, as seen by the amount of text devoted, is out of proportion relative to the other Gospels. Nothing like it appears anywhere else in them, even if taken cumulatively.
2. List all of the political terms in v. 1. This is in keeping with earlier "historical" references to the birth of Jesus' during the reign of Caesar Augustus and the administration of Roman policy in Syria by Governor Quirinius (2:1–2).
3. The citing of the Jewish religious leadership in v. 2 follows the orientation to the temple and its personnel with which the Gospel opens in chapters 1 and 2. Is this indicating the priority of the religious over the political (as is the sequencing in Zechariah 3–4 of Joshua the High Priest ahead of Zerubbabel, the Davidite in the restored, post-Exilic community)? The Book of Ezra, the priest, precedes that of Nehemiah, the governor, during that same era.

4. Luke's greater citation of Isaiah 40:3–5 also exploits the Way of the Lord language in its itemizing of extensive and thorough engineering activity. What, practically speaking, is gained by lopping off mountains and hills, filling valleys, straightening the crooked, and smoothing the rough ways? As earlier observed in note 4 of the "Preface," early believers were known as belonging to or following after "The Way [of the Lord]" in Luke's second volume.
5. What did such attention to detail imply for Luke's readers regarding their setting in "history"—both sacred and secular?
6. To what extent should the modern interpreter and student frame his own personal story and that of his "people" within the broader context of the church's past, its current setting, and that of the future?

6

Luke 3:8–14 & Matt 3:8. Fruits Worthy of Repentance in L & Q

Goal

To display the dramatic differences between Luke and Matthew regarding the content and context of John the Baptizer's preaching. In so doing, one sees further evidence of his redactional agenda. One is also in a position to determine the significance that Luke, through the words of John, attributes to his preaching.

Luke 3:8–14	Matt 3:8
1. "fruits worthy of repentance" (8)	"fruits worthy of repentance"
2. sharing clothing (11)	
3. sharing food (11)	
4. financial integrity (12–13)	
5. avoiding extortion, threatening violence; contentment with wages (14)	

1. Both Matthew and Luke (l. 1, Q) report John's exhortation to "bear fruits worthy of [= equivalent to] repentance"—that is, if one has truly repented, then several results of equal worth/value were to come about. While Matthew does not specify them, Luke does (vv. 10–14: L again). What behaviors were to follow calls to repentance in your experience? Mine were largely limited to reading the Bible, prayer, witnessing, church attendance, and "personal" purity. Of course, this is not to deny the virtues of such endeavors. Rather, they do not comport with the Baptizer's/Luke's standards.

2. Why would the audience regard the content of John's proclamation as messianic (3:15, L only)?
3. Lest one confine John's message exclusively to the realm of "ethics" or "social justice," how does Luke regard it (v. 18, L only)? This should help to resist the tendency to drive a wedge between theology (or gospel) and ethics so apparent in curricular distinctions between the two.[1]
4. How does the L material here correspond to emphases in L material included elsewhere in this Gospel? Recall Mary's song in 1:52–53? Fast-forward to Plot 31: the story of Zacchaeus in relation to John's preaching (19:1–10).
5. What is to be made of such frequency and consistency?

1. Axiology (from the Greek word ἄξιος used by Luke at 3:8) is the study of values in ethics.

7

Luke 3:23–38 & Matt 1:1–17. Jesus' Genealogy

(Compared & Contrasted)[1]

Goal

To highlight the special features of Luke's genealogy, both in relation to its structure and placement within the framework of the entire Gospel but also its distinction vis-à-vis Matthew's genealogy. It is a good place to observe how each Evangelist adopted, adapted, and arranged (i.e., "redacted") his material—whether oral or written.

	Matthew 1:1–17	**Luke 3:23–38**
1. Location	Beginning of Gospel	Between baptism & temptation
2. Content	Since Abraham David's reigning, royal "sons" 4 Notorious (Gentile) women	Prior to Abraham, since Adam David's non-reigning, royal "sons" [elsewhere: righteous (Jewish) women]
3. Scope	Fewer: generations omitted	More numerous (seventy-seven) —before Abraham —after Exile
4. Pattern	3 x 14 generations	none
5. Sequence	Earliest to latest (forwards)	Latest to earliest (backwards)
6. Age	None	About 30
7. Title	"Son of David, Son of Abraham"	["Son of Adam"]

1. The differences are too great to regard both as belonging to Q material.

1. Extended genealogical lists available to each Evangelist occur in 1 Chron 1:1—2:1–15, 3:5–12 and Ruth 4:12–22. It is not clear how much Luke and Matthew drew on other oral or written traditions.

2. Gentiles, technically speaking, are all the generations between Adam and Abraham in Luke's genealogy. Although Matthew begins his list with Abraham, they are not absent from his version. All four women, who would have been considered "of ill-repute,"[2] were non-Israelite.

3. Although Luke's list does not contain any women in Jesus' lineage, he more than makes up for the exclusion by the number and role of women that he includes throughout his Gospel, especially at the outset.

4. Luke's genealogy is fuller, both in taking the genealogy beyond Abraham to Adam and by including more generations between the Exile and Jesus.

5. Their placement is different, as is their sequence. What is the more usual position of a genealogy?

6. What is one forced to do, and what is gained, by placing it between the baptism and the temptation accounts? What word/theme is being stressed as a result?

7. What is different about Luke's and Matthew's list of David's heirs—of whom the king had many via four wives and additional women in the harem?

8. Can one make a distinction between *royal* sons (who were numerous) and *reigning* sons—those who occupied the throne? Although only Matthew lists the latter, might Luke's list be "saying" that, although he did not reign from his father's (= ancestor's) throne, Jesus was nevertheless also a son (= descendent) of David? Or, put another way, Jesus (great David's greater Son) need not have occupied the *political* throne to have been his heir. Consequently, non-reigning royal sons are stressed. (By the way, it must be recalled that David was known for other qualities besides exercising political authority and waging war.) What was the point of listing the royal, though not reigning descendants?

2. Of course, the men involved would have to be charged with moral failure as well. Ruth, a Moabite, has in her ancestry the daughters of Lot who committed incest with their father (Gen 19:30–38).

9. My hunch (which would require textual/archeological evidence) is that the Nathan listed as David's immediate heir in Luke's list (3:31) was one of the sons whom, according to 2 Sam 8:18, their father appointed as priests (כהנים, αὐλάρχαι, *sacerdotes*).[3] This double legacy (Jesus as both king and priest) would accord with both the royal and priestly temple-cultic themes that saturate the early chapters of the Third Gospel.[4]

10. Both Matthew and Luke concur that Shealtiel was the father of Zerubbabel, a descendent and political leader of Jews who had returned to Judah from Exile in Babylon. However, he governed at the pleasure of the Persian king (rather like Herod under the current Roman regime). The prophet Zechariah authorized Zerubbabel's joint rule with Joshua, the High Priest (chapters 3–4), God referring to them both as "sons of oil"—i.e., as anointed (messianic?) ones—"who stand before the Lord of all the earth" (4:14).

11. Matthew's abbreviated (he skips generations) and structured pattern—3 sets of 14[5]—may signify that Jesus was the ultimate or supreme descendent of Abraham and David (14 being a multiple of 7 which, with 3, suggest perfection or completeness).

12. Should it be objected that both genealogies end (Matthew) and begin (Luke) with the davidite, Joseph (whom both Evangelists take pains to maintain was not Jesus' biological father), one can make the case that adoption could confer name, property, and rights then as now.

13. This is the only place in the Bible where Adam is regarded as God's son.[6]

14. Although scholars do not agree about how deliberate Luke was at this point, what is the potential significance of having "Adam" immediately precede the Q account of Jesus' desert temptation/testing, the Devil asking, "If you are God's Son, . . ."?

3. My suggestion must remain at the level of informed speculation, based upon several other intriguing appearances of "Nathan" in the OT.

4. This educated guess is fleshed out in my article "Role of Nathan."

5. There are actually two sets of 14 and one of 13, since David ends the first set and begins the second. King Jeconiah ends the second and begins the third.

6. Although the usual word for "son" (υἱός) is not used here (as it was at the beginning of the genealogy in v. 23), the genitive singular of the definite article serves throughout the list to indicate this familial relationship more briefly.

15. John Milton, in his lesser-known epic poem, "Paradise Regained" (Book I, ll. 1–7), regards this desert testing as the great reversal to Genesis 3, already accomplished by Jesus at the *beginning* of his ministry:

    I who erewhile the happy Garden sung,
    By one man's disobedience lost, now sing
    Recover'd Paradise to all mankind,
    By one man's firm obedience fully tried
    Through all temptation, and the Tempter foil'd
    In all his wiles, defeated and repuls't,
    And *Eden* rais'd in the waste Wilderness.[7]

    And later (Book 4, ll. 606–15):

    . . . now thou has aveng'd
    Supplanted *Adam*, and by vanquishing
    Temptation, hast regain'd lost Paradise,
    And frustrated the conquest fraudulent:
    He never more henceforth will dare set foot
    In Paradise to tempt; his snares are broke:
    For though that seat of earthly bliss be fail'd,
    A fairer Paradise is founded now
    For *Adam* and his chosen Sons, whom thou
    A Savior art come down to reinstall, . . .[8]

16. In Luke's thinking, is it possible to be the Son in status or identity only? How important is the Son's role or task (understood as obedience)?
17. St. Paul develops this concept more fully in Romans 5.

7. Milton, *Complete Poems*, 483, italics his: here and following.
8. Milton, *Complete Poems*, 529.

8

Luke 4:5–8[1] & Dan 7:13–14. A Tale of Two Visions

Goal

The influence of Daniel (esp. chapters 2 and 7) upon the Gospels has been profound, particularly so far as their theology of the kingdom of God and Son of Man is concerned. It is the purpose of this Plot to show how much the LXX of Daniel 7 has contributed to the vocabulary and theology of the Temptation narrative. This enables one to view the testing of Jesus (and one's own?) within a broader, apocalyptic context—thereby increasing the stakes of what is involved.

	Daniel 7:13–14	**Luke 4:5–8**
1. Who? DONOR	Ancient of Days	Devil
2. To Whom? RECEIVER	one like a son of man	Jesus
3. What? GIFTS	gave [διδ–]	will give [διδ–]
a.	kingdom [βασιλει–]	all kingdoms [βασιλει–]
b.	glory [δοξ–]	glory [δοξ–]
c.	authority [εξουσια–]	authority [εξουσια–]
d.	worship [λατρευ–]	worship [λατρευ–]
4. Where? PLACE	Babylon	Desert, Judea (Roman occupation)
5. When? TIME	Distant past Eschatological	Near past "Historical"

1. Vetne, "Influence and Use of Daniel," 33–35 largely cite the parallels, but not in this manner.

	Daniel 7:13–14	Luke 4:5–8
6. By Whom? AUTHOR	Daniel the Prophet/Seer	Luke the Evangelist
7. How? GENRE	Apocalyptic dream	"Historical" narrative

1. The parallel (Q) at Matt (4:8–9) omits "authority" from the Devil's offer.
2. Reflect on the (un)conditionality of the bequests in Daniel 7 and Luke 4.
3. Weakened by fasting so long, Jesus' condition corresponds to an understanding of the son of man idiom to mean, "frail, vulnerable human."
4. Professor Christopher Rowland has called my attention to Luigi Schiavo's "The Temptation of Jesus," 141–64. The author cites Daniel 7 among many other texts (biblical and otherwise) in support of his argument that the temptation of Jesus by Satan represents in Q the earthly counterpart of an eschatological struggle occurring in the heavenly realm. However, it is my contention that this chapter plays a much larger role in influencing the dynamics and vocabulary of that encounter, especially in Luke's adaptation of the material. Furthermore, Schiavo cites Daniel 7 only briefly and in other respects, and not the LXX of it. He might have argued that vv. 13–14 recount the rewards of victory, the spoils of war, as it were. Q emphasizes the conditions by which they are to be won.
5. Is it fair to say that, according to Matthew and Luke, Satan in the Gospel offers to Jesus that which the Ancient of Days grants to the son of man figure in Daniel—on different terms? Does this realization "up the ante" of testing, regardless of the subject?
6. For a detailed account of how the terms in 3a–d of the display help one to demonstrate the literary and theological unity among chs. 1–6 of Daniel and between them and ch. 7, see my "Daniel and the Three," 43–61.

9

Luke 4:13. Sonship: Announced, Declared, Listed, Tested

Goal

To illustrate how Luke in the first four chapters adopts, adapts, and arranges his sources to convey a particular understanding of Jesus' sonship and (by implication) of those who belong to God's family.

Announced to Mary (L) (1:32)	**Declared at Baptism** (TT)[1] (3:22)	**Listed in Genealogy** (L)[2] (3:23a)	**Tested in the Desert** (Q) (4:1–13)
"the Son of the Most High"	"my Son, the Beloved"	"the son (as was thought) of Joseph"	"If you are the Son of God" (3)
		son of (23b . . .)	"If you are the Son of God" (9)
		son of	
		son of	
		77 times	
		"Adam, the son of God" (38)	

1. For convenience sake (and to avoid an extended foray into source criticism), I employ the (so far) prevailing theory about synoptic relationships: Luke and Matthew adopted, adapted, and arranged Mark's

1. Among the details added to this common material is "historical" information (L) about local political and religious rulers in "Luke, the 'Historian' (2 of 2)."

2. See the separate study of the genealogies in Luke and Matthew (Plot 7).

Gospel, their shared common material (Q), and traditions peculiar to each (L and M).

2. What was Luke forced to do by placing his genealogy here rather than at the beginning of ch. 1 (as Matthew does)? What did the Evangelist gain by such a move?
3. Judging by the criterion of frequency alone in the first instance, at what theme is Luke hammering away? How did he achieve this emphasis, particularly in the last three columns, whose contents follow so closely on one another?
4. Is it enough for Jesus to have been conceived, declared, and authenticated as God's son? What does this imply for all of God's adopted sons and daughters? Put another way, is being a child of God (having status and identity as such) sufficient?

10

Luke 4:1–13 & 11:1–4. Desert Testing/ Temptation & the Lord's Prayer

Goal

The vocabulary and subject matter in these passages is too similar to be ignored. The exercise below seeks to interpret them (each adaptations of Q) in their intermediate and near contexts. As result, perhaps one can arrive at a more precise understanding about the nature of the "trial." In Plot 25, the relationship between 11:2 and 20 is explored more fully.

	Temptation/Testing (Ch. 4)	**The Lord's Prayer** (Ch. 11)
1	"was led" (1)	"do not bring us" (4)
2	"forty days" (2)	"each day, daily" (3)
3	"he was tempted"	"to the time of trial" (4)
4	"by the devil"	[evil, the evil one]
5	"bread" (3, 4)	"bread" (3)
6	"all the kingdoms" (5)	"Your kingdom come" (2)[1]
7	"the Lord your God" (6)	"Father"

1. A similar comparison can be drawn between Matt 4:1–11 and 6:9–13. The latter is fuller in that "evil/the evil one" is present. Some manuscripts of Luke contain the bracketed material in l. 4, the copyists

1. I have long felt, based on the suggestion of one of my first-year Greek students, that the opening two petitions (grammatically imperative in the third person singular) could be rendered more forcefully in English. Her insight would justify translating v. 2, "Cause your name to be hallowed, cause your kingdom to come." This would make their force parallel with, "Give us this day," etc. in vv. 3–4.

perhaps wishing to align both prayers more closely. Satan and demons do figure prominently a few verses later (11:18–20).

2. The words for "tempted" and "trial" are similar in Greek (πειράζειν, πειρασμός). So, the vocabulary of l. 3 is actually closer between the two than the NRSV allows.

3. With this in view, is it possible to infer the nature of the temptation/trial that the petitioner seeks to avoid? Is it testing of a general kind? Or, is her/his concern of a particular sort?

4. Did Luke mean his readers to understand that the petition of 11:2 was answered by Jesus' action and statement in v. 20—"But if it is by the finger of God that I cast out the demons, then the kingdom of God has come to you"?

5. Has this profound and stunning announcement been fully appreciated and acted upon by readers?

11

Luke 4:16–21. The Nazareth Sermon in Isaianic & Levitical Contexts

Goal

To exploit the terminology of this passage in its own right and to show how important the Bible in Greek (of both Testaments) is to a deeper appreciation of the message that Luke's Jesus conveys in their light.

Isa 61:1–2 (LXX)	Luke 4:16–21
1. "The Spirit of the Lord is upon me	"The Spirit of the Lord is upon me
2. because he has anointed me; he has sent me	because he has anointed me
3. to bring good news to the poor,	to bring good news to the poor.
4. to heal the brokenhearted,	
5. to proclaim	He has sent me to proclaim
6. release to the captives	release to the captives
7. and recovery of sight to the blind	and recovery of sight to the blind,
8.	to let the oppressed go free,
9. to summon the acceptable year of the Lord	to proclaim the year of the Lord's favor."
10. and the day of retribution	
11. to comfort all who mourn. . . ."	

1. Both passages (ll.2–3) directly link the anointing—or making "messiah"—(ἐκρισέν με) to the task of bringing good news to the poor. Luke relates it to Jesus as God's Christ (Χριστός). Some interpreters might see here ingredients for a later Trinitarian theology: Spirit, Lord, Anointed One (Christ).

2. The sending to proclaim release to the captives (ll. 5–6) is more directly connected to Jesus in Luke. This task was assigned to God's people in Isa. 58:6.

3. Luke doubles the reference to liberation (ll. 6 & 8). In each case, the normal word for "release/let go" is used: ἄφεσις.

4. While scholars routinely note that "The Acceptable Year of the Lord" or "The Year of the Lord's Favor" (l. 9) (δεκτός in each case) refers to the Year of Jubilee (Leviticus 25), few if any connect Jesus' stress on liberation with the Septuagint's rendering of the Hebrew יובל (*juval*) ("shouting, blowing") by ἄφεσις: "The Year of Release [ἔτος ἀφέσεως]." While the vocabulary of "release" occurs in the Hebrew of Leviticus 25, there is no direct verbal connection with "Year." We rely on the LXX for that.

5. Behind the phenomena of Leviticus 25 lies Deuteronomy 15, which stipulates that poverty is to be eliminated by adopting the system of the "sabbatical year." Every seven years, debts, indebted laborers, and the land must be released. In the fiftieth year, an additional release has to occur: the land must be returned (with compensation) to those among whom it was originally allotted. God owns the land. His people are tenants and aliens (vv. 22–24). They own the crops and herds that it produces and sustains. None can accumulate and hold acreage in perpetuity so as to become a "land lord," thereby lording it over others.

6. Furthermore, it is rarely noted that the Jubilee Year / Year of Release was to begin on the Day of Atonement (v. 9). On this occasion, a live goat was to be released (ἀφιέναι) into the desert bearing away the People's sins (Lev 16:10). So, comprehensive liberation was envisioned: from sin, from landlordism, from debilitating indebtedness, and from slave-labor. The land was to be freed from production. So much more was to take place than allowed by the ditty, "I have a Jubilee down in my heart." The stress is upon individual liberation: "Since Christ has set me free, I have a Jubilee; I have a Jubilee down in my heart." There is nothing here of the communal and economic character of Levitical Jubilee and its eschatological fulfillment by the Lukan Jesus.

7. Historical treatments take into account certain DSS texts that look forward to a messianic figure to proclaim such a message of

liberation.[1] However, it is really the LXX that provides the immediate canonical and theological context for the Lukan account and for Christian readers.

8. While scholars debate the extent to which Jubilee was practiced, the theological point must not be lost sight of. The issue is not Israel's (dis)obedience but the will of God for the people. What did God intend? At the base of communal ethics lies theology.

9. Such comprehensive liberation is grounded upon divine saving action and command: God's deliverance/release of Israel from political and economic slavery in Egypt and the authority as Savior to require the liberated to act accordingly.

10. Scholars regularly point out that Jesus omits any reference to retribution (l. 10). He also avoids the distinction between Judah, who are to be called "priests of the Lord and ministers of God" (v. 6a) and the aliens and strangers who will feed Judah's sheep and maintain its agriculture (v. 5). And God's people are to inherit the nations' wealth (v. 6b). Little wonder then that Jesus' congregation reacts with murderous intent when he interprets the fulfillment of Isaiah's prophecy (v. 21) as extending Jubilary benefits to the Gentiles (vv. 24–30).

11. Since the meanings of ἀφίημι/ἄφεσις are so different in English translations at 4:18–19 and 24:461–47, could we say that the former presupposes Jubilary Atonement, while the latter takes for granted the Jubilary ethics of release (and that Acts 2 & 4 combine the two)? See the separate Plot 40: "Luke 24:46–47 & 4:16–18. Jubilary Forgiveness & Release. One Kerygma or Two? Apples & Oranges?"

12. So far as I am aware, only one branch of Ante-Bellum American Methodism (later termed "Free Methodism") made these passages the textual basis of their liberationist reform movement. Although the themes were announced as early as 1860, the text itself was expounded in print by the Rev. Benjamin T. Roberts four years later.[2]

1. See especially these studies that take into account the nature and extent of Jubilary themes in Luke (Sloan, *Favorable Year*) and in the SG and Acts (Ringe, "Jubilee Proclamation").

2. Roberts, "Gospel to the Poor."

12

Luke 4:25–27. Signs & Wonders: Jesus, Elijah, & Elisha

Goal

Two extremes need to be avoided in general when comparing and contrasting Jesus with Jewish and Greco-Roman figures: claiming too much or too little about him. This is particularly so in the case of miracle working. What should be made of the fact that Elijah and Elisha performed the same kind of mighty works attributed to Jesus? Accuracy and precision are required when citing similarities and differences.

	Elijah	Elisha	Jesus
1. Nature miracle	Heavy rain (1 Kgs[1] 18:41–46)		Storm calmed (8:22–25)
2. Food multiplied		100 fed (2 Kgs 4:42–44)	Thousands fed (9:10b–17)
3. Leprosy cured		Naaman healed (2 Kgs 5:13–14)	10 lepers cleansed (17:11–19) [L]
4. Dead raised			
—a. daughter			Jairus's daughter (8:40–56)
—b. son	Widow's son (1 Kgs 17:17–24)	Parents' son (2 Kgs 4:32–37)	Widow's only son (7:11–17) [L]
5. Exorcisms	-0-	-0-	SG: multiple examples, FG: none
6. "Ideology"	Not explicit	Ditto	Kingdom of God drawn near

1. The NETS labels this book "3 Reigns" and the following one as "4 Reigns"—1 and 2 Reigns standing for 1 and 2 Samuel. The LXX titles this material βασιλείων: "of the kingdoms."

1. It is good to be reminded that the basic meaning of prophet (as this is derived from the Greek, πρό + φημί) is "one who speaks on behalf of [God]." The classic prophets (of which Elijah and Elisha are representative) did not so much foretell the future as they did "tell forth" the word of God to the present—the response to which would have consequences: immediately, soon, or later.

2. Given the divinely endowed capacity of these *human* prophets to perform such cures, is it legitimate to use them as proofs of Jesus' *divinity*? In the case of 3 and 4.b., the people give glory and praise to God for what Jesus had done (7:16, 17:15, 18).

3. Of course, if one focuses on quantity (How many?) rather than quality (What kind?), it could be said of #1–4a, that Jesus himself did more of the same than Elijah and Elisha combined.

4. Luke reproduces cures of leprosy found in the other SG. However, here, L provides a ten-fold increase in the number cleansed (#3, above). One was a Samaritan, hailing from territory that had been occupied by the Syrian officer Naaman (2 Kgs 5:13–14), whom Elisha had cured of leprosy. With Mark and Matthew, Luke recounts the story of Jesus' previously healing a leper (5:12–16).

5. By supplying (#4.b.) the unique account (L) of widow's *only* son (a designation unused in the other passages), Luke doubles the number of times in the Gospels that Jesus himself raised someone from the dead. By including it, he also matches the two reports of Elijah's and Elisha's separately doing so. See Plot 19 for 7:11–17. Might the implied message be, "A greater than Elijah and Elisha is here!"?

6. #5: no prophet was ever credited with performing exorcisms—yet another kind of healing and related to the coming of God's kingdom. See Luke 10:9 and 11:20, where the connection among cures, exorcisms, and the kingdom of God is explicit (#6).

7. What can be concluded about the function of miracles in Luke? What do they "say" about Jesus' status and role?

13

Jesus & Asclepius: Healers Extraordinaire

Goal

The purpose of this exercise is to evaluate claims that Luke and the other Gospel accounts portray Jesus in "colors" that have been borrowed from the larger Greco-Roman world. As elsewhere in this book, comparing and contrasting basic categories are meant to provide an accurate, comprehensive, and systematic approach to evaluating the significance of similarities and differences.

	Jesus	Asclepius
1. **What? (Event)**	Cure of illnesses	Cure of illnesses
2.	Exorcism of demons	
3. **Conditions**	None/once: faith (in God)	Some (pre- or post-)
4. **Response(s)**	Nothing tangible	Presents, inscriptions
5. **To Whom? (Subject)**	Praise to God	Praise to Asclepius
6. **Where? (Place)**	Anywhere (except temple)	Temple of Asclepius
7. **When? (Time)**	Anytime (except at night)	At night
8. **(Occasion)**	Publicly (usually), privately	Privately, during dream
9. **(Ideology)**	Kingdom of God	(Universal good)

1. Perhaps the most widely known healer in the ancient world was the divine-man Asclepius (sometimes spelled "Asklepios"). His activity is often put forward by scholars as a model from which the Gospel writers drew when portraying the role of Jesus as healer. However, such claims must be evaluated by closer analysis, which the Plot above helps to conduct. These data hold true for healings in the

other Gospels and for exorcisms in the SG. (Not a single expulsion of demons/unclean spirits occurs in the FG.) See C & D, *Documents*, 151–52 for the texts, which I have selected because these inscriptions clearly predate the Gospels. Kee (*New Testament in Context*, 144–46) provides a somewhat-expanded collection of the material, with variations in translation that, however, do not affect the point being made here. Dittenberger's critical edition of the originals remains standard.

2. As always, the dating of such parallels must be attended to: as contemporary or earlier than the gospel accounts. This is where the instances collected by C & D (even in the latest edition of 1994) must be examined carefully. Few of their samples come with dates (even approximate ones). One would have to be able to rule out the possibility that at least some examples from the Greco-Roman world might have been influenced by Gospel accounts.

3. Harvey in *Jesus and the Constraints of History* (115–17) has observed that, among healing narratives throughout the ancient world, it is Jesus who is reported in the Gospels to have performed the most cures among the paralyzed, blind, deaf, and mute. In the Jewish world, no one has been reported as doing so. Thus, among his contemporaries, he was unique in this regard. Furthermore, these four constitute most of the healings within the Gospels themselves. In the light of Isa 35:5–6, what might Jesus or the Evangelist be implying with such a concentration of these particular miracles—especially if they had addressed congenital conditions, in some instances, at least?

4. While Jesus accepts the occasional expression of faith that he or God can perform the cure (category 3), he never requires it as a precondition. (The demon-possessed are themselves incapable of such respsonsiveness.) And, in the SG, faith is never *in* Jesus (as it is in the FG). Nor does Jesus ever expect thanks or require those healed to follow him as disciples. Only once (the case of Blind Bartimaeus) is it said that a cured person followed Jesus—and that on his own initiative (Luke 18:43 and parallels). Indeed, Jesus declares that Bartimaeus's faith had been the means of restoring his sight (v. 42). However, he had not made it a condition. What do such phenomena imply, so far as the concept of grace is concerned?

5. Although Jesus is certainly the agent of these demonstrations of power, their source is always God, who is also the subject of praise given

by the cured and astonished onlookers (as in v. 43). What is the case with Asclepius?

6. While the differences in most of the categories above are obvious, that of ideology (#9) is more subtle. One must look to such telltale texts as Luke 9:1–2 and 10:9 to make the distinction.
7. At the end of the day, one can say that these similarities reflect elements of a shared paradigm used by writers in the Greco-Roman world in their accounts of notable persons. However, the kind of differences noted point to a particularly Christian variation in the contents of the common pattern.

14

Luke 5:17–26. The Paralytic's Descent—and Ascent

Goal

To observe how Luke adapted details in this account, found in all three SG, in view of his readers' cultural circumstances.

	Matt 9:1–8	Mark 2:1–12	Luke 5:17–26
1. **Materials**	none recounted	[mud-packed branches]	tiles [κέραμοι] (19)
2. **Action**	none recounted	"removed the roof . . ." "having dug through it" (4)	[removed]

1. Matthew does not mention lowering the paralytic through the roof to access Jesus.
2. Palestinian roofs were built with tree branches packed with mud. Serious damage would have to be done to create an opening large enough for a man-bearing stretcher to be lowered: hence, Mark's more destructive expression. Tiles ("ceramics") were more commonly used throughout the Hellenistic world.
3. Mark's account reflects the local Palestinian color, whereas Luke's version speaks to a wider audience.
4. What does this suggest about the freedom exercised by the Evangelists to shape/adapt/modify their traditions to suit the readers' needs/situation? Could this process apply to ideas as well as construction materials?

15

Luke 6:17, 20–36. The Beatitudes

(Q & the Dead Sea Scrolls)

Goal

To illustrate the significance of Luke's version of common tradition (oral or written) regarding blessedness, with an eye to the Dead Sea Scrolls. The Matthean and Lukan texts are quoted (from the NRSV, as usual).

Dead Sea Scrolls (Hymn 9)[1]	**Matthew 5:1–12 (on the Mountain)**	**Luke 6:17, 20–36 (on the Level Place)**
Members of the Qumran community	Disciples (1)	Disciples (20a)
"causing all the well-loved poor	Blessed are the poor in spirit,	Blessed are you who are poor,[2]
to rise up together from the trampling"	for *theirs*[3] is the kingdom of heaven. (3)	for yours is the kingdom of God. (20b)
	Blessed are those who mourn,	Blessed are you who weep now,

1. Vermes, *Dead Sea Scrolls in English*, 179. All of the lines quoted from it are in succession. This shows that "those eager for righteousness" (as in Matthew) and "the well-loved poor" (as in Luke) belong to the same group. That the latter designation bears an economic dimension (as in Luke) is supported at the opening of the Hymn, where "poor" is in the company of "the fatherless." Wycliffe's Middle English translation (ca. 1394) of Matthew 5:3 seems to combine the two conditions: "Blessed ben pore men in spirit." See *The English Hexapla*.

2. The Greek reads, "Blessed are the poor."

3. Although not reflected in English translations, in the second line of each Matthean Beatitude, the third person plural personal pronouns in Greek are emphasized (hence my italics). This implies a contrast: not the exalted in spirit, the happy, the haughty, the full, etc. Luke, of course, makes the contrasts explicit.

Dead Sea Scrolls (Hymn 9)[1]	Matthew 5:1–12 (on the Mountain)	Luke 6:17, 20–36 (on the Level Place)
	for *they* will be comforted. (4)	for you will laugh. (21b)
	Blessed are the meek,	
	for *they* will inherit the earth. (5)	
"those eager	Blessed are those who hunger and thirst	Blessed are you who are hungry now,
for righteousness"	for righteousness,[4] for *they* will be filled. (6)	for you will be filled. (21a)
	Blessed are the merciful,	
	for *they* will receive mercy. (7)	
	Blessed are the pure in heart,	
	for *they* will see God. (8)	
	Blessed are the peacemakers,	
	for *they* will be called children of God. (9)	
	Blessed are those who are persecuted	Blessed are you when people hate you
		and exclude you, revile you, and defame you
	for righteousness's sake,	on account of the Son of Man (22)
	for *theirs* is the kingdom of heaven. (10)	. . . for surely your reward is great in heaven
		But woe to you who are rich,
		for you have received your consolation. (24)
		Woe to you who are full now,
		for you will be hungry. (25)

4. Wycliffe renders *iustitiam* as "rightwiseness," suggesting an orientation more than a state or condition.

Dead Sea Scrolls (Hymn 9)[1]	Matthew 5:1–12 (on the Mountain)	Luke 6:17, 20–36 (on the Level Place)
		Woe to you who are laughing now, for you will mourn and weep. Woe to you when all speak well of you, for that is what their ancestors did to the false prophets. (26)

1. The audience addressed by Jesus in Luke consists of people from everywhere; however, at v. 20a, he identifies a particular group within it: "Then he looked up at his disciples." This focus upon his followers is reinforced by references to the prophets in vv. 23 and 26. See #6 and 9, below.
2. While Matthew's use of the third person makes the statement more universal (and in a sense removed), what does Luke's use of the second person pronoun (plural in Greek) accomplish?
3. Meekness and poverty of spirit need to be thought of in theological rather than psychological terms. A "personality profile" is not being promoted. (Pride in being a lowly worm or a doormat leans towards pathology.) Rather, the opposite of arrogance before God and others is in view. According to Numbers 12:3, Moses—who liberated Israel from slavery in Egypt—was the meekest of all men (the LXX and Matthew use the same Greek word).
4. When, in both versions, Jesus calls blessed those who endure abusive language and bodily harm, he puts them in the same company as the prophets (5:10–12//6:22–23). This association will be particularly significant in the Woes that follow Luke's extended version.
5. On the whole, which Evangelist puts the stress upon interiority and the private? Who emphasizes the economic and physical?
6. In the case of Luke, whose condition is being addressed, given the audience (v. 20a) and the citation of the prophets? Does this make the

reference to poverty and hunger less universal? Is blessedness in this instance a condition of all or of Jesus' student-followers?

7. The same questions need to be asked of the woes in Luke (vv. 24–26). Is Jesus attacking/lamenting the condition of the affluent among the general population, given the reference (yet again) to false prophets? These are religious people whose special role it was to speak on God's behalf.

8. Do such data support or challenge the notion that the Beatitudes are entry requirements into the kingdom of God? Keep in mind that, both in the case of Matthew and Luke, the audience of disciples consists of those who had been previously called by Jesus. They had not come to him out of their own initiative. So, all interpretations of these attitudes and actions as being somehow meritorious are unfounded.

9. The question arises in both instances (5:11–12//6:22–23) as to why those expressing these characteristics and behaviors should suffer persecution and abuse? Might it be that they are actually much more revolutionary and provocative towards social, political, and commercial norms (and leaders) than is generally allowed?

10. Note the "gaps" in each version. Do they correspond to that which each Evangelist "says" throughout his Gospel?

11. I attempt a biblical theology of such similarities and differences in the following Plot.

16

The Beatitudes in Luke & Matthew

Biblical Theology as Dialog/Dialectic /Point-Counterpoint

Goal

To suggest a way of valuing and using both accounts of Jesus' teaching about the nature of blessedness, as this is rendered uniquely by Luke and Matthew.

	Matthew	Luke
	Attitude	Activism
	Being	Behavior
Confirmation	*Interiority*	Exteriority
	Subjectivity	Objectivity
	Individual	Group
	Private	Public
	Activism	*Attitude*
	Behavior	*Being*
Challenge	Exteriority	*Interiority*
	Objectivity	*Subjectivity*
	Group	*Individual*
	Public	*Private*

1. The objective is to avoid harmonization, preferential treatment, and reductionism—these being a denial of the approved diversity bequeathed to us once the process of canonization became coalesced.

2. Of course, the big question is "How?" What manner or means should be employed? If not harmonization, preferential treatment, or reductionism, then where can one turn?

3. A way to proceed is to assume that each text performs two functions: it confirms one audience or outlook (point); and it challenges another audience or perspective (counterpoint). To support as well as to critique is the property of each text. The interpreter is charged with determining which suits the needs of a particular circumstance. The following is but a suggestion of the way that one might proceed.

4. Inner and outer weather[1]

    a. Matthew's account challenges an activism insufficiently concerned with right attitude. Luke's version challenges right attitudes that never get expressed in action.

    b. Matthew questions a behaviorism that is not grounded in being. Luke raises doubts about being in the right without behaving in a corresponding manner.

    c. Matthew forces one to attend to one's interior weather, lest external manifestation be merely superficial. Luke brings up short those whose concern for inner purity leads to a navel gazing that has no outward counterpart.

    d. Matthew warns against objective manifestation unrelated to subjective experience. Luke counters an understanding of subjective experience that is insufficiently expressed in the concrete and tangible.

    e. Matthew sees a danger in much of communitarianism, wherein the individual is lost in the group. Luke protests against a "Lone Ranger" super individualist mentality that ignores the socially constituted nature of healthy individual development. (Even the Lone Ranger always traveled in the company of Tonto.)

    f. Matthew qualifies a rampant tendency to show and tell all to as many people as will listen rather than cultivating a private quietness and security—in one's closet. Luke resists a privatization of spirituality, which is a denial of the great public acts of God in

1. It was Aldous Huxley who referred to George Herbert as "the poet of this inner weather." See his *Texts and Pretexts*, 13.

history, open to all who have eyes to see—as demonstrated on the Day of Pentecost in volume two.

5. Of course, one can find the opposite qualities throughout each of the two Gospels. My point is limited to the Beatitudes and to the Thesis-Antithesis dialectic of Matthew 5 and the less-structured versions of them in Luke 6.

6. This very often depends upon context. In my teaching experience, Evangelical audiences have found support in Matthew's understanding of discipleship but have been challenged by Luke's. Liberal audiences have expressed just the opposite responses.

17

Luke 6:27–36 & Matt 5:43–48. Loving Enemies

Goal

To compare and contrast both Gospels so as to demonstrate the significance of their resultant similarities and differences on this distinctive teaching of Jesus about the nature and scope of divine love.

Matthew 5:43–48 (from the mountain)	Luke 6:27–36 (from a level place)
1. "Love your enemies (44).	"Love your enemies (27), [See v. 35.]
2.	***do* good** to those who hate you,
3.	bless those who curse you,
4. Pray for those who persecute you,	pray for those who abuse you." (28).
5.	Striking cheeks, taking coat & shirt (29)
6.	Giving to beggars, letting go of goods (30).
7.	"***Do*** to others as you would have them ***do*** to you" (31).
8. so that you may be children of your Father in heaven; (45).	["you will be children of the Most High; (35a).]
9. for he makes his sun rise on the on the evil and on the good, and sends rain on the righteous and on the unrighteous.	[for he is kind to the ungrateful and the wicked" (35b).]
10. For if you love those who love you, what reward do you have?	"If you love those who love you, what credit is that to you?
11. Do not even the tax collectors ***do*** the same? (46)	For even sinners love those who love them" (32).

Matthew 5:43–48 (from the mountain)	Luke 6:27–36 (from a level place)
12. And if you greet only your brothers	"If you ***do* good** to those who ***do* good** to you,
and sisters, what more are you ***do***ing than others?	what credit its that to you?
Do not even the Gentiles ***do*** the same?" (47)	For even sinners ***do*** the same" (33).
13.	"If you lend from those from whom you hope to receive, what credit is that to you? Even sinners lend to sinners to receive as much again" (34).
14.	"But love your enemies [See v. 27.], ***do* good,**
	and lend, expecting nothing in return" (35).
15. Be perfect, therefore,	"Be merciful, just
as your heavenly Father is perfect" (48).	as your Father is merciful" (v. 36).

1. Italicized and bold letters are mine. I have quoted Matthew in full (and Luke for the most part, excepting vv. 29–30, ll. 5–6) according to the NRSV.
2. Overall, who employs the language of doing more? Who stresses the need for doing good? It is not the case that Matthew entirely ignores doing good. Rather, he makes the point in different terms (as Luke does, too). God's children should imitate their divine Parent who showers the rain upon the good and evil, who shines the sun on the righteous and unrighteous (v. 45).
3. How, according to the contexts of both passages, should "love" be defined? Is anything said about subjectivity, feeling, or emotion?
4. Since loving enemies is enjoined twice (at both Luke 6:27 and 35 [#1 & 14]), who are the subjects of everything in between—including "Do to others as you would have them do to you" (v. 31)? Matthew places his version of the "Golden Rule" in an entirely different section of his Sermon (7:12).

5. In the case of the Matthean context, define "perfect"/"complete" (v. 48) in relation to the Father's actions towards the two classes of humankind (#8–9). Do the same for Luke 6:36.

6. Without denying the differences between "perfection" and "mercy" in the final verses, might the common point be that each must be extended to all constituencies? In the case of Luke, the extending of mercy must not be limited (imperfect/incomplete) to those like us.

7. When observing such an array of differences, keep in mind that we have before us several possibilities. As is the case with general pedagogical experience, Jesus himself might have adapted a fundamental message to different audiences and occasions, depending on the needs. Or, these are two different renditions of a single sermon, adapted by the interests of those who passed on the teachings as well as modified by each Evangelist according to his aims.

8. Often neglected, so far as the terminology of "love" in the OT is concerned, is the injunction to love the stranger as oneself (Lev 19:33–34)—perhaps because one stops reading after the oft-cited, "You shall love your neighbor as yourself" in v. 8. The theme of doing good even to the enemy can be found at Prov 24:17–18 and 25:21–22. However, behaving in such a manner is not cast in terms of loving him/her.

18

Luke 7:1–10 & Matthew 8:5–13. The Centurion's Servant

Goal

To observe how Luke maintains his redactional agenda by comparing and contrasting yet another instance of shared material. This is the first of three passages about healing, which the Evangelist uses to build into a crescendo that leads up to John the Baptizer's query about Jesus' identity.

	Luke 7	**Matthew 8**
1. **WHERE? Placement**	After Sermon on Plain	After Sermon on Mountain
2. **WHO? Protagonist**	Centurion	Centurion
3.	—Worthy[1] (4)	
4.	—Unworthy[2]: twice (6–7[3])	—Unworthy[3] (8)
5. **WHO? (2)**	Centurion's servant[4] (2)	Centurion's servant[3] (5–6)
6.	—"valued highly"	
7. **WHAT? Health crisis**	—"ill and close to death"	"paralyzed, in terrible distress" (6)
8. **WHO? (3) Agents**	Jewish delegation (3)	Centurion himself goes to Jesus (5)
9.	Centurion's friends (6)	
10. **HOW? Manner/means**	"But only speak the word" (7)	"But only speak the word" (8)

1. ἄξιος

2. οὐ . . . ἱκανός εἰμι, οὐδὲ ἐμαυτὸν ἠξίωσα (Luke 7:6–7); οὐκ εἰμὶ ἱκανός (Matt 8:8)

3. The NRSV omits this part of v. 7, even though the manuscript support for it is strong.

4. παῖς ("servant," "son") and δοῦλος ("slave," "servant") are both used in each version.

	Luke 7	Matthew 8
11.	Faith/belief > Israel (9)	Faith/belief > Israel (10)
12. WHAT? (2) Result	"in good health" (10)	Cure, healed (7, 13)
13. SO WHAT? Significance	["eat in the kingdom of God"][5]	"eat . . . [with patriarchs] in the kingdom of heaven" (11)

1. Whose diagnosis of the slave's illness is the more dramatic (#7)?
2. In both instances, the central figure (after Jesus), is a foreigner—a Gentile member of the occupying Roman army and therefore an enemy.[6] Might Luke have in mind Jesus' example of Elisha's curing the Syrian officer, Naaman (cited by Jesus in 4:27), whose army had been making forays into Northern Israel (2 Kings 5)—the territory roughly corresponding to Galilee?
3. Matthew's Centurion initiates the contact with Jesus on behalf of his slave (#8, v.5), whose close relationship Luke highlights (#2). How does this begin to underscore the officer's reticence according to the Third Evangelist?
4. What is to be gained by the Centurion's double confession of unworthiness in Luke, even after the Jewish delegation (initiating the appeal to Jesus on his behalf) describes him as worthy (#s 2–4)?
5. Unlike Naaman, the Syrian officer, Luke's Centurion enjoys mutual regard with the occupied Jews. In 6:27–35, Jesus had taught his disciples to love their enemies by doing good to them. Are the tables being turned here when the enemy "loves our nation and has built us our synagogue" (v. 4)? The so-called "Good Samaritan" practices a similar kind of reversal (10:25–37), the point almost always missed when strangers helping strangers in need are identified thus.
6. Although in this instance and several others, faith that Jesus possesses the authority and ability to perform the cure (#10–11)[7] appears as a

5. Luke places this saying at 13:28–29.

6. See also the reputation of the Italian centurion Cornelius in Acts 10:1–2, who is described as being devout—one who feared God with his household. He prayed to God and gave to the Jewish poor. Peter preached a sermon to this Gentile audience reminiscent of his sermon at Pentecost to Jews during the Feast of Pentecost (vv. 34–38).

7. The expression "believing in(to)" (πιστεύειν εἰς) Jesus is confined to the FG and to

condition, there is an equal (and perhaps greater?) number of cases where he practices prodigal (not random) acts of grace. This is especially so with regard to exorcisms, where the possessed are in no condition to respond with mind and will. How rarely does one hear preachers and expositors point to the times when he heals unconditionally: not requiring either faith or repentance to gain forgiveness, nor demanding that one follow him.

Matt 18:6, where the comment is made privately to a circle of disciples about tripping up vulnerable members of the community.

19

Luke 7:11–17. Raising the Widow's Son from the Dead (L)

Goal

In this exercise, the purpose is to examine more closely an account of resuscitation, unique to the Third Evangelist (L). Because Elijah and Elisha are reported to have done the same, it is important to compare and contrast this passage with those accounts to see accurately wherein the similarities and differences lie. This should also help one to understand Jesus' response to John the Baptizer's query that follows (vv. 18–23). The OT texts have been reversed for heuristic purposes. As always, all three passages need to be read in full first.

	Elisha (2 Kgs 4:32–37)	**Elijah (1 Kgs 17:17–24)**	**Jesus**
1. **Dead child**	Parents' son	Son (among others)	Son (only)
2. **Mother**	Married, wealthy[1] woman of Shunem	Widow of Sarepta	Widow of Nain
3. **Setting**	Private: house	Private: house	Public: town gate, great crowd
4. **Demography**	Israel	Gentile & outside of Israel	Jewish & within Israel
5. **Method of healing**	Partial body contact, prayer	Full body contact, prayer	Touching bier, speaking
6. **Agent's identity**	Woman: "man of God"	Woman: "man of God"	Crowd: "Great prophet"

1. So the NRSV translates גדולה אשה at v. 8. The LXX renders it γυνὴ μεγάλη: "a great woman" (NETS).

1. Following on the cure of the Centurion's servant, who was *near* death, Luke dramatically provides an account of an *actual* one.
2. With this insertion of L material, the Evangelist doubles the SG accounts (the other: the raising of Jairus's daughter). The FG contains two resuscitations as well; but they are different subjects: a synagogue ruler's son and Lazarus.
3. Although all three stories relate dire circumstances, which is the greater—given the status of both mother and son (#1 and 2)? Where are the stakes higher, personally and economically? Could this be why Luke recounts that Jesus "had compassion for her" (7:13)? The Greek word σπλαγχνίζεσθαι connotes deep, visceral reaction. It occurs in the Third Gospel only two other times: in the emotion directed by the Good Samaritan towards the stricken traveler (10:34) and that of the father towards his repentant, returning younger son (15:20).
4. While the private setting (#3) in the OT is "reported out," being made public to the reader, of what significance is the public setting in Luke?
5. Whose story (#4) displays "the wideness of God's mercy"—which Jesus cites in the L material of 4:25–26.
6. Whose method of healing (#5) is the most authoritative? If the features of Plot 12 are also taken into account, then Luke might be saying indirectly that "a greater prophet than Elijah and Elisha is here."
7. So far as the healers' identity is concerned (#6), Elijah and Elisha (both prophets) are each further identified as "man of God."[2] Is it a sign of restraint that Jesus is acclaimed by the crowd "only" as "a Great Prophet" rather than as "Christ" or "Son of God"? Luke and John each make six references to Jesus as such a spokesperson for God (Matthew and Mark each making three). So, it is apparently a significant one for the Third and Fourth Evangelists. Could conservative Christians risk down-playing this category, fearing that one might regard him "merely" as such?
8. Do you find it significant that, while *Jesus* performs this miracle, the audience praises and glorifies *God*, claiming that God has "looked

2. Although the NETS has "man of God" at 17:18, it changes the same Greek expression to "a divine man" at v. 23. However, both here and at v. 18, the LXX reads ἄνθρωπος θεοῦ not θεῖος ἀνήρ. For a standard analysis of the latter expression, see Holladay, *Theios Aner*.

favorably upon[3] God's people" (v. 16)? The theocentric nature of Jesus' words and deeds should not be ignored nor minimized.

9. This general reservation about drawing messianic conclusions regarding Jesus is manifested even by John the Baptizer, whose query (via emissaries) comes next: "Are you the One who is to Come, or shall we look for another?" Is this expression an upgrade from "prophet" to "the Prophet Like Moses" who is to come (Deut 18:15–19)?

10. Such uncertainty should come as no surprise since, throughout the SG, Jesus does not proclaim himself publicly as the Son of God or the Messiah, nor does he let others (including both humans and unclean spirits) do so. He prefers the more ambiguous (even ironic) "the Son of Man."[4]

3. The RSV (in contrast to the NRSV) translates ἐπισκέψεσθαι as "visited," an idea associated with God's intervening or saving the people.

4. For a useful survey regarding the interpretation of this expression, see Burkett's *Son of Man Debate*.

20

Luke 7:18–23 & Matt 11:3–6. Jesus' Reply to John the Baptist

Goal

Both Evangelists share a version of the exchange between emissaries of the imprisoned prophet and Jesus. His question and Jesus' response are tabulated below in the context of healings predicted in Isaiah 35 (and 29). In this way, one can visualize better the ramifications of Luke's additions regarding estimates of Jesus.

Isa 35:5–6	Matthew 11	Luke 7
1.	"Are you he who is to come, or shall we look for another?" (3)	"Are you he who is to come, or shall we look for another?" (19)
3.		"Are you he who is to come, or shall we look for another?" (20)
5.		"In that hour he cured many of
6.		diseases and plagues and evil spirits and many that were
7. blind see	blind receive sight (5)	blind he bestowed sight." (21)
8. lame leap	lame walk	lame walk,
9.	lepers cleansed	lepers cleansed
10. deaf hear	deaf hear	deaf hear
11.	dead raised up	dead raised up
12.	good news preached to the poor [πτωχοί][1]	good news preached to the poor [πτωχοί][1] (22)

1. Isaiah 29 also looks forward to a time when the deaf will hear and the blind see (v. 18). Furthermore, it adds that "the meek shall obtain fresh joy in the Lord, and the neediest people [LXX: πτωχοί, as in the Gospels, above] shall exult in the Holy One of Israel" (v. 19).

Isa 35:5–6	Matthew 11	Luke 7
13.	"Blessed is he who takes no offense at me." (6)	"Blessed is he who takes no offense at me." (23)
14. speechless sing[2]		

1. According to Luke (v. 18), John's disciples had reported "all these things"—most recently, the raising in Nain of the widow's only son from the dead, where the people had exclaimed, "a great prophet has arisen among us" and that "God has visited his people." Might this be a reference to "the one who is to come"?
2. What is the effect of Luke's doubling the question from John (ll. 3–4)?
3. What is the effect of l. 5?
4. Which condition is not mentioned, either in Isaiah 35 or in Matthew's version (l. 6)—though it is throughout the SG (but never in the FG, nor the HB for that matter[3])?
5. What do both passages imply, so far as Isaiah 35 is concerned? Is one of the messages that Jesus goes beyond the expectations (more than fulfills) of that prophet?
6. What might account for the Baptist's apparent disillusionment? Recall his preaching about the Coming One (3:15–18).

2. Mark alone records Jesus' cure of the mute (7:37; 9:17, 25).

3. However, demonic possession/harassment does occur throughout the book of Tobit in the GOT.

21

Luke 9:1–6, 10:1–22 & Testament of Levi 18.[1]

The Twelve & Seventy(-Two)[2] Authorized & Sent

Goal

To set Jesus' authorization of his student-followers within the context of Second Temple expectations held by at least some Jews during this era. Careful attention to detail again guards against over- and underestimations about Jesus' status and role.

	T. Levi 18:2–3, 12	Luke 9:1–6 (and TT)	Luke 10:1–22 (L)
1. Who?	New [royal] Priest	Jesus	Jesus
2. What?	authority to trample on	power & authority to cast out	given authority (19)
3. Whom?	Beliar shall be bound		over all the power of the Evil One (19)
	wicked spirits	all demons & to heal diseases	demons & spirits subject in Jesus' name (17, 20)
4. By Whom?	"his 'children'"	the Twelve	the Seventy(-two)
5. So What?	?	God's kingdom proclaimed	God's kingdom drawn near (9, 11)
6. When?	future	present	present
7. Where?	unknown	the villages	every town & place (Galilee)

1. For the text, see Kee, "Testament of Levi," 778, 794–95; or Kee, *Origins of Christianity*, 178; or Charles, *Apocrypha and Pseudepigrapha*, 314–15.

2. Manuscripts of ancient Bibles of similar quality are evenly divided regarding the precise number of those sent.

1. The passage in question tells of a figure's bearing the marks of a royal priest, about whom this is said (vv. 6–7): "The heavens will be opened, and from the temple of glory sanctification will come upon him, with a fatherly voice, as from Abraham to Isaac. And the glory of the Most High shall burst forth upon him. And the spirit of understanding and sanctification shall rest upon him [in the water]." The resemblance to Gospel accounts of Jesus' baptism are noted by many; and virtually all commentators regard the bracketed phrase as a Christian interpolation. However, the judgment may be premature, for Matthew and Mark recount the vision and audition as occurring after Jesus had left the water. Neither Luke nor John mentions the water at all.
2. We have seen that Jesus' being a descendent of David is set in the context of temple persons and activity in chapters 1–2, reminiscent of the king-like figure in l. 1 (T. Levi 18:2–3).
3. The parallel at Matt 10:1 says nothing about the kingdom of God. Mark 6:7 says that Jesus "was giving [the Twelve] authority over the unclean spirits." They preached that people should repent and "were casting out many demons and were anointing many sick with oil and they were healing" (vv. 12–13). In the original call of the Twelve, Jesus intended to send them preaching and "to have authority to cast out the demons" (3:14–15). There is no mention of kingdom preaching or enacting occurring in either place. Apparently, it was Luke's special concern to do so (l. 5) by doubling the emphasis.
4. Luke 9 (ll. 2–3) expands the scope of the Twelve's authorization; and its range increases with the seventy(-two) in ch. 10.5. No significance in terms of God's Rule is cited in T. Levi (l. 5). However, it is perhaps implied by Beliar's being bound by the New (Royal) Priest (l. 3, v. 12a). In 11:20, Jesus' own exorcistic activity seems to cause the God's kingdom to arrive (in answer to the prayer of v. 2?), not "merely" to draw near (as in l. 5).
5. Is it too far-fetched to suggest that Luke is "doubling down" on this expectation among certain circles during the Second Temple era—that the anticipated figure has indeed appeared in Jesus?

22

Luke 10:18. Satan's Fall (L)

Goal

To demonstrate that there is more than one option for reading a statement about a past event, especially where the language of apocalyptic eschatology may need to be considered.

	"I watched"	**"Satan fall from heaven . . . ."**
Long Ago?	Before the incarnation?	Before creation?
Recently?	During his lifetime?	At the temptation?

1. This statement is unique to the Third Gospel.
2. Was the Lukan Jesus (or the Jesus of pre-Lukan tradition) claiming to have observed a primordial event in a pre-incarnate state?
3. Does the Lukan Jesus (or the Jesus of pre-Lukan tradition) claim to have seen an event occurring during his lifetime: e.g., following the temptation?
4. Was this meant to be an assertion regarding a "real time" event? Or did an experience occur in a revelatory vision, complete with characteristic symbolism (as with the author of the Apocalypse at ch. 12:10, where the expulsion [ἐκβάλλειν] of Satan occurs during the Christ event)?
5. My *Navigating Revelation* (47–48) displays and discusses several accounts of Satan's fall in extra-canonical literature in connection with ch. 12.

23

Luke 10:25–28. The Parable of the "Good" Samaritan (L)

Goal

By displaying an overview of the essential differences among the SG rendering of the commands to love God and neighbor, one is able to get a sense of the Evangelists' distinctive concerns. None are more evident than in Luke, with his adaptation of TT material and with his inclusion of L material.

Matt 22:34–40	Mark 12:28–34	Luke 10:25–37
1. Lawyer: the Great Commandment?	Scribe: the First Commandment?	Lawyer: doing → eternal life? (25)
2.		Jesus: what does the Law say? (26)
3. Jesus: love God & neighbor	Jesus: love God & neighbor	Lawyer: love God & neighbor (27)
4. Law & Prophets hang on them	Scribe: loving God & neighbor supersedes cultus	
5.	Jesus: nearness to God's kingdom	Jesus: do & live (28)
6.		Lawyer: who is my neighbor? (29)
7.		Jesus: Parable of Good Samaritan
8		Jesus: who proved [RSV] neighbor? (36)
9		Lawyer: one who showed mercy (37)
10.		Jesus: do likewise

1. It is not unusual for a common tradition to be placed differently by the Gospel writers and to have various interlocutors. In this case, Luke sets the dialog during the Travel Narrative—the other Evangelists agreeing on Jerusalem. In Mark, a scribe engages Jesus; Matthew and Luke make him out to be an expert in the Law (#1).

2. Although the two commandments to love God with one's entire being and to love neighbor as oneself are already known in the OT (Deut 6:5 and Lev 19:18[1]), it is in the later Jewish tradition (The Testaments of the Twelve Patriarchs) that they are joined for the first time (T. Dan 5:3; T. Issachar 5:2, 7:6). Perhaps that is why Luke does not feel compelled to credit Jesus for the union (#3). However, identifying them as fundamental to the Law (Matt 22:40), superior to the cultus (Mark 12:33), and the way to eternal life (Luke 10:28) is unique to the Gospels (#4 & 5).[2]

3. Are you surprised at Jesus's response to the lawyer's initial question in Luke (#1 & 2)? Is it not odd, according to conventional evangelistic methods, that he does not say, "That's your problem. You think that good works will earn you salvation! Instead, repent of your sins and believe in me"?

4. Is it further surprising to those Christians schooled in being against the Law (or being very suspicious of its value), that Jesus suggests that the answer lies in the very Law of which he is an expert (#2): that, in so doing, he will live (#5)?[3]

5. Here, as in so many instances, we encounter "what might be called Lordship Christology" or "Lordship soteriology." There is no reference to the death of Jesus. Rather, it is his authoritative word that is effective (a soteriology of the Word?).

1. Often missed is that God also commands Israelites to love the stranger as oneself, their having experienced being strangers in Egypt (Lev 19:33–34).

2. For a fuller treatment of each emphasis, see Lemcio, "Gospels and Canonical Criticism," 119–21.

3. See the separate consideration of the parable about the rich man and Lazarus (also L), where Jesus takes the same tack (16:19–31): the former's ultimate destiny lay in his failure to obey that which Moses and the prophets (cited twice) taught about treating the poor. Again, there is no christological self-reference—apart from Jesus' authority to say so. Is this enough evidence about a soteriology of the Word for those reading the Gospels through lenses ground according to a certain interpretations of other NT texts and colored by a particular dogmatic theology?

6. In the parable (L material), Jesus once again engages in reversal thinking with the citation of the Samaritan's acts of compassion. Tally the number of steps taken to care for the victim, ignored by both priest and Levite. The savior figure belonged to a people despised for seven centuries as cultural and religious half-breeds (2 Kgs 17:24–41) and as opposed to the temple's rebuilding after the Exile (Ezra 4). Amy-Jill Levine points to the mutual hostility between Samaritans and Jesus' disciples in the near context of 9:51–56.[4]
7. What does the language of "proving" (RSV) or "becoming"[5] (#8) suggest about the identity, place, and status of "neighbor"?
8. For the second time, Jesus commands action (#10). How much does behavior count within relationships in general and saving relationships in particular? Is "being" (or having the right attitude) alone ever sufficient?
9. Are you surprised that Jesus does not require the lawyer to follow him, to become a disciple? This "neglect" occurs more often than one might think.

4. Levine, "Many Faces," 24, 68.
5. γεγονέναι. The NRSV has "was."

24

Luke 11:1–4 & Matt 6:9b–13. The Lord's Prayer[1]

Goal

To appreciate the nature of Luke's shorter version in the light of Matthew's fuller and better-known one. Study in connection with Plot 25 for the Lukan context.

Luke 11	Matthew 6
1. "Father, (2)	"Our Father in heaven,
2. hallowed be your name.	hallowed be your name. (9)
3. Your kingdom come.	Your kingdom come.
4.	Your will be done,
5.	on earth as it is in heaven. (10)
6. Keep giving* us day by day* (3)	Give us this day
7. our daily bread.	our daily bread. (11)
8. And forgive us our sins (4)	And forgive us our debts,
9. for we ourselves are forgiving*	as we also have forgiven
10. everyone indebted to us.	our debtors. (12)
11. And do not bring us to the time of trial."	And do not bring us to the time of trial,
12.	but rescue us from the evil one." (13)

1. I have departed from the NRSV at these points* so as to reflect more adequately the sense of the Greek.

1. One might be tempted to ask, "Why bother with Luke's shorter, "thinner," version when one has Matthew's" (the basis for the church's liturgical use)?
2. Did Luke abbreviate (ll. 3–5) because he assumed that the coming of God's kingdom would include the comprehensive (earth + heaven) doing of God's will?
3. What is Luke's concern regarding supply (l. 6)? Does this suggest anything about the Evangelist's understanding of salvation history as being "for the long haul"?
4. The NRSV's alternative reading, "our bread for tomorrow" (l. 7), may be requesting a guaranteed supply: tomorrow and tomorrow and tomorrow. However, some interpreters have understood the petition eschatologically—the prayer for God's kingdom to come and (in the case of Matthew) the testing (πειρασμός) both being references to that final, world-wide trial from which the church at Philadelphia is to be spared (Rev 3:10).
5. Eugene Peterson's translation of the Matthean petition (l. 7) in *The Message* is based upon a use found in a mother's grocery list among the Oxyrhynchus Greek papyri discovered during the late 1890s in ancient Egyptian trash heaps: "get today's [= fresh, not yesterday's] bread."[2]
6. Are you surprised that the petition for a physical need precedes that of a spiritual one? One hears Salvation Army workers say, "You can't preach the gospel to someone with a toothache."
7. Note that the English rendering "forgive" is the usual word for "release" or "let go" in Greek (ἀφίημι). Does this give more insight into the nature of forgiveness? What is often said to someone's obsessing over a real or perceived wrongdoing?
8. Although the offenses needing forgiveness in Matthew are limited to debts (sins of omission), Luke includes sins of commission (ll. 8–10). What does the continuous action of the Greek verb suggest?
9. Is there significance to the sequence/order of forgiveness? In other words, when/at what point does Father forgive? Is this an example of the dreaded "works righteousness?"

2. For a thrilling account of their discovery (illustrating something of the "romance of classical and biblical scholarship"), see Parsons, *City of the Sharp-Nosed Fish* and the popular summary in Patterson, "Oxyrhynchus Papyri."

Note that, in both versions, the entire Sermon (as well as in this prayer), Jesus addresses those whom he had *already* called to be his disciples. The initiative is always God's.

10. Do the first two petitions (ll. 2 and 3, above)—about the hallowing of God's name and the coming of God's kingdom (Matt 6:9–10//Luke 11:2)—seem to be rendered rather feebly in most translations, preceding as they do the more robust appeals for bread and forgiveness? Yet, all are expressed in the Greek imperative mood. Many years ago, in raising the translation challenge to a class of intensive beginning Greek, a (regretfully now-anonymous) student suggested that they be translated causally: "Cause your name to be hallowed; cause your kingdom to come." Despite her newness to the subject, she showed what is possible when an alert mind catches the significance of a grammatical point and applies it to a particular text.

11. Just 18 verses later in Luke, Jesus explains the significance of his exorcising activity: "If I by the finger of God cast out demons, then the kingdom of God has come upon you." Is this saying (set in a different context at Matt 12:28) intended to be the fulfillment of the petition in v. 2? Or is 11:20 the inauguration (the "already") of the future (the "not yet") for which one is to pray?

25

Luke 11:2–4. The Lord's Prayer in Immediate Context (vv. 5–20)

Goal

To demonstrate how context plays a crucial role in determining interpretation—in this instance, the nature and timing of the kingdom's coming.

The Lord's Prayer	The Immediate Context
"Father," (2)	"heavenly Father" (13)
hallowed [ἁγιασθήτω] be your name.	"Holy Spirit [πνεῦμα ἅγιον]"
Your kingdom come."	"kingdom" (twice in vv. 17–18)
	"The kingdom of God has come to you" (20).
"give" (3)	"give" (5 times in vv. 9–13)
"bread" (4)	"bread" (5, 11)[1]
"forgive [ἀφίημι]": "loose," or "release"	"cast out [ἐκβάλλειν]" (6 times in vv. 14–20)

1. The contexts for the Matthean and Lukan versions of the Prayer are entirely different. So, their diverse placements are deliberate and need attention.
2. That kingdom language occurs four times within eighteen verses of chapter 11 suggests the significance and connection among the

1. Major velum manuscripts of the mid-fourth century are divided regarding the originality of the reference to giving bread (which the NRSV omits). Two papyrus manuscripts from the previous century lack any mention of the expression.

statements. This is especially the case with the kingdom's coming in vv. 2 and 20. Might the latter declaration be the answer to the former petition? If so, how futuristic is the Evangelist's timing of this event?

3. More than any other synopticist, Luke frames Jesus' ministry within the context of a struggle between the reign of God and the reign of Satan. His exorcism of the demons is cited as evidence of it.[2]

4. We saw in the previous Plot that "release" should be understood behind the English rendition of the Greek as "forgiveness." When Jesus casts out demons, he releases victims from their control.

5. So far as the timing of Jesus' invasion of Satan's household is concerned, to which event in the past does the present perfect of the verb (in both Greek and English) point? When was the previous occasion during which Jesus encountered the Devil? What, then, was the nature and result of that experience?

6. Access both to release from sins and freedom from demonic oppression belongs to the experience of comprehensive liberation resulting from the coming of God's rule in Jesus.

7. As much as the two examples of bread supplied to the importunate friend requiring bread—and to the son asking his father for it—are meant to be instances of God's provision, there is the phenomenon of humans supplying one another with the needed nourishment. Although the heavenly Father is the source of nourishment, it is intermediate agents who provide it on a day-to-day basis, as well as during emergencies.

2. Not a single exorcism occurs in the FG; nor is the kingdom of God ever the subject of Jesus' *public* preaching and teaching. The expression does occur twice in the *private* encounter between Jesus and Nicodemus (3:3, 5). For a display and discussion of these and other remarkable differences between the two gospel traditions, see Lemcio, *Soaring*, 1–3.

26

Luke 11:21–22. The Parable of the Strong(er) Man

Goal

To examine the internal structure of this saying to determine its meaning in Luke and to set it within the background of eschatological thinking held by some Jewish groups during the Second Temple Era.

Implication (a)	**The Parable**		**Implication (b)**
(1) SATAN	**(2) Strong Man**	**(3) Stronger Man**	(4) JESUS
Demonically controls	Fully armed	Assails, overcomes[1]	Exorcizes demons
	Guards palace	Takes away armor	
People possessed	Goods at peace	Divides spoils	People freed

The Lukan Context

1. The elements of the parable are displayed above in (2) and (3). It is possible to infer the intended meaning in (1) and (4).
2. All three SG (the TT) record Jesus' response to the accusation that he is in league with Satan and the demonic. However, Luke's is the fullest, being double the others in length. It follows Jesus' stunning statement (found also at Matt 12:28) about the timing of God's Rule and the

1. The Greek νικᾶν ("conquer" or "overcome") occurs twenty-seven times in the NT: once here in Luke (nowhere else in the SG), once in the FG (16:33, with Jesus as the conqueror, but in a totally different context), and sixteen times in Revelation.

manner of its arrival: "If I by the finger of God cast out demons, then the kingdom of God *has come* upon you" (v. 20, italics mine).[2]

3. Might this also be regarded as at least a partial answer to Luke's rendition of the Lord's Prayer ("May [or 'Cause'] your kingdom [to] come") just 18 verses away (v. 2)? Matthew's version of the saying (12:28) appears seven chapters distant from his account of the Prayer (6:9–13).

4. This expanded treatment of the encounter corresponds to the Third Evangelist's fuller portrayal of Jesus as exorcist, as shown by the entries in a concordance for "demon" and "unclean spirit" and by the concentration of this subject within chapters 9–11. Such a cluster of terms for kingdom-related exorcisms occurs most fully in Luke.

5. In this connection, see the earlier study of Luke 10:18 in Plot 22.

6. Given the present perfect tense of the verb (both in Greek and English), when had the victory over Satan occurred? What was the original encounter between the two? Does this inform one's understanding of that experience?

Second Temple Judaism

7. Review Plot 21 for the study of Luke 9:1–6, 10:1–22 & Testament of Levi 18. The relevant portion of this text reads, "And Beliar shall be bound by Him, and He shall give power to His children to tread upon the evil spirits" (v. 12).

8. Of the four instances in the HB or in the Protestant OT (which, since the sixteenth century, corresponds to it in content), none portrays Satan as head of an army of demons opposing God and God's people.[3] Nor are there any accounts of possession by unclean spirits—of the kind found in the SG and Acts. But they do occur in the writings of the Deuterocanon (a more neutral term than "Apocrypha"), which are present in the LXX and Bibles of the ancient church, being recognized

2. Not a single exorcism is reported in the FG. Nor is the kingdom of God the subject of Jesus' *public* preaching and teaching there. He does use the expression *privately* in the nocturnal encounter with Nicodemus (3:3, 5). For a display and discussion of this and other differences, see Lemcio, *Soaring*, 1–3.

3. In Job 1:6 & 2:1, he has access to a gathering of "sons of God" (HB or "angels of God" in the LXX). A *satan* ("accuser" or "adversary") or *diabolos* ("slanderer") in 1 Chron 21:1 and Zech 3:1–2 need not be supernatural agents.

by Roman Catholic and Eastern Orthodox Christians since then. See especially Tobit 3:17; 6:8,14–15; and 8:3.

9. The view of Satan as head of an opposing force of fallen angels who became demonic spirits occurs most frequently in books of the so-called "Pseudepigrapha" ("false inscription/attribution"—especially Jubilees 5, 7, 10; 1 Enoch 6–16; and the Life of Adam and Eve 12–17).[4] The use of the more prejudicial term, "Pseudepigrapha" (whether employed by scholars or a dominant religious party), obscures the fact that at least some of this literature was regarded as authoritative by the groups that preserved them during the Second Temple Era. In the NT, Jude 14 (in another connection) cites 1 Enoch 1:9 as a prophecy uttered by the ante-deluvian ancestor.[5]

10. Is it legitimate to conclude that at least some of Jesus' contemporaries, were ready to accept that these anticipated events were taking place during (and because of) his ministry?

11. If so, what may one conclude about the influence of this "intertestamental" literature upon the thinking of Jesus, the synoptic Evangelists, and the author of Revelation (esp. chapter 12)?

4. See Lemcio, *Navigating Revelation*, 47–48 for a display and discussion of these texts in light of the HB and Revelation 12.

5. Jubilees and Enoch appear between 2 Chronicles and Ezra in the Ethiopian Orthodox OT.

27

Luke 14:15–24 & Matt 22:1–14. The Great Banquet & Wedding Feast

Goal

To ascertain the distinctive points of Luke, vis-à-vis the Matthean account[1] *in parables that, though they are similar in significant ways, are substantially different in others. At issue are inclusivity and exclusivity, unconditionality and conditionality.*

	Matt 22:1–14	Luke 14:15–24
Subject	About the kingdom of heaven (2)[2]	About the kingdom of God (15)
1. Who?	King	Master of the house (16, 21)
2. What? (1)	Gave wedding banquet for son	Gave great banquet
3. Whom? (1)	Originally invited[3] twice (3–4)	Many originally invited (16)

1. It is not necessary to determine whether these versions represent (1) an original that Jesus himself adapted on separate occasions for the benefit of different audiences, (2) a single, earlier tradition, radically rendered in different directions by each Evangelist to meet the needs of his readers, or (3) one Gospel writer's adapting and arranging the other for the requirements of his congregation.

2. The expressions "the kingdom of God" and "kingdom of heaven," are equivalent ones—as the immediate context of Matthew indicates (21:43). The issue is one of origin, not place: not where God rules, but whence God reigns. Matthew's overall tendency to use "heaven" is thought to reflect Jewish sensibilities about the divine Name: employing a circumlocution to avoid profaning it—making it a common, ordinary expression without special significance. Pious Christians (and others without religious scruples, so far as language is concerned) still say, "Heaven help you, if you do that again!" or "Good heavens!"

3. The Greek καλοῦν can also be translated "call," enabling some interpreters to discern a larger theological meaning.

	Matt 22:1–14	Luke 14:15–24
4. **What?** (2)	Ignore, kill servants (5–6)	All decline (18–20)
5. **What?** (3)	King destroys city (7)	Master angry at originals (21)
6. **What?** (4)	Compel others (8)	Bring, urge others (22–23)
7. **Whom?** (2)	Good & bad (9–10)	Poor, crippled, blind, & lame
8.		People from highways & alleys
9. **What?** (5)	Inspection, exclusion (11–13)	Rejection of originals (24)
10. **Whom?** (3)	Guest without wedding garment	
11. **So What?**	Many called, few chosen [on condition] Like kingdom of heaven (2)	

1. Since I have dealt in some detail with the much-discussed historical and redactional issues (including the "extreme" and exaggerated measures taken by the meals' hosts and guests),[4] I will not repeat them here. Instead, my aim is to frame the lesson in terms of the immediate and remote contexts of each text: imitate God (Luke); imitate the guests (Matthew: presumably, all but the one had come prepared with the garment).
2. It is not surprising that Luke's secondary guest-list should include the marginalized (ll. 6–8, vv. 22–23), whom he has specially featured in earlier modifications of material common with Matthew and in his appropriation of L material.
3. Luke's account is immediately preceded by questions about whom to invite for meals. James A. Sanders has noted that the guests in this parable are the very ones, according to one of the Dead Sea Scrolls (1QSa II, 5–22), who are to be entirely excluded from the Messianic Banquet.[5] Given the Third Evangelist's concern to elevate the marginalized and to warn the rich and powerful of their downfall, is it surprising that the former were not (among) the first to be invited?
4. Matthew's conditionality (for *remaining*, not entering) is reflected in the immediately preceding parable (TT) of the Wicked Tenants,

4. See Lemcio, "Parables of the Great Supper and the Wedding Feast," 1–26.
5. Sanders, *God Has a Story Too*, 86–87.

which ends with the kingdom of God's being given over to a nation "making/doing its fruits" (21:43)—that is, responding appropriately: better than the original leaders had.

5. How much does Matthew say about the son? Is he active at all? Does this mean that there is no Christology here—except for Jesus' saying so? Is this sufficient? Be sure to keep track of similar Lukan instances of alleged christological and soteriological "deficiencies."
6. Although Matthew's parable is the more unconditional, so far as members of the secondary guest list are concerned (the good and bad in vv. 9–10), in what sense is Luke's unconditionality greater?

28

Luke 15. Parabolic Ingredients & Dynamics

Goal

To determine the nature and significance of Luke's adopting, adapting, and arranging (= redacting) Q and L material and to suggest an intra-parabolic function for this threefold cluster.

Sheep	Coin	Son
Animate subject	Inanimate object	Personal subject
Shepherd	Woman (God)	Son
Divine initiative	Divine initiative	Human Response (repentance)

1. See the next plot to detect the nature and significance of Luke's adapting Q regarding the derelict sheep.
2. It is (among other things) the function of the third parable to provide an example of **human** response since the first two are about **divine** initiative.
3. With the parable about the younger son, we get a sense of what it means for the sinner **to repent.** Such human behavior (prompting joy among the heavenly angels) cannot be illustrated by an animal (sheep) nor an object (coin).
4. Although the third parable might rightly be called "the Prodigal Father" because of the generous welcoming of the returning son, does Luke recount the Father's searching high and low for him (as do the shepherd and woman for their lost items)? Could it be that the focus is more on "anthropology"—on responsibility—on the son's "coming

to himself" and acting on it? Is there a complementary expectation for the older brother?

5. Does this final parable about feasting because of the returned son also help to identify more precisely the tax collectors and sinners with whom Jesus was eating (v. 2)—those who had repented? This of course does not imply that he avoided unrepentant tax collectors and sinners.
6. Given the conditions ascribed to the younger son by the father and brother at the end of the parable, how else might "lost" and "found" be understood?
7. There is something profoundly poignant in the status of the older brother in the father's household and relationship. Is this a case of being "so near and yet so far?" What had the younger son found that the elder brother had never lost?

29

Luke 15:3–7 & Matt 18:10–14. The Parable of the Lost/Stray Sheep

Goal

To demonstrate how Luke and Matthew render and arrange Q in keeping with their redactional agendas. Is the former more "evangelistic" and the latter more "pastoral," as is sometimes claimed? Once more, precise attention to details is critical.

Categories	Luke 15	Matthew 18
1. Audience(s)	Public: tax collectors & sinners (1)	Private: disciples (1), the church [ἐκκλησία] (17)
2. Context	Pharisaic & scribal critique (2)	"despising one of these little ones" (10)
3. Agent	"one of you" (3)	a shepherd (12)
4. Sheep: number	100	100
5. Sheep: condition 1	*Lost* (3x)	*Stray/wander* (3x)
6. Sheep: location	Wilderness (4)	Mountains (12)
7. Owner's response (a)	Leaving the 99 (= "righteous persons") (4, 9)	Leaving 99
8. Owner's response (b)	Seeking and finding the *lost*	Finding the *stray*; one of "little ones" (10, 14)
9. Joy expressed	by the man, friends, neighbors, heaven (6–7)	man rejoices over the 1 more than the 99 (13)
10. Condition 2	*repentant sinner*	*little one* not *lost* (14)
11. Emphasis	"Evangelistic": for the world?	"Pastoral": for the church?

1. We have here two possibilities (as in other instances) for the origination of Q material: either a single parable was adapted to different settings by Jesus himself, or the Evangelists themselves are responsible for the modifications and placements according to their distinctive redactional agendas.
2. As we saw, the Lukan parable about lostness, unlike the Matthean, is reinforced by two further examples of the same condition: of a coin (vv. 8–10) and of a son (vv. 11–31).
3. *About* whom (given vv. 10 and 14) is the Matthean version written? *To* whom is it given?
4. Is Matthew's emphasis (10, 14) a surprise, given his concern for the community/assembly (ἐκκλησία) of disciples: their entry, status, assignment, discipline, and wholeness?
5. Does this mean that Jesus' audience in Luke is broader: those still outside the circle of his followers?
6. Jansen (*Exercises*, 94) observes that the Gospel of Thomas interprets the shepherd's motive for seeking the lost sheep because of its being the largest of the flock. Although the author does not cite its location, this saying occurs in logion 107. Nor does he point out that the parable concludes with yet a further implied motive: "I love you more than the ninety-nine" (Aland and Aland, *Synopsis*, 829). Funk, *New Gospel Parallels*, 184, translates the first clause as "I care for you . . . ."
7. Although the Lukan version seems to be more "evangelistic" and the Matthean version more "pastoral," are such categories meaningful in each context? In neither case is the lost/wandering sheep an outsider per se. Was it not one of the 100? Perhaps this is the real distinction, given to whom Luke's version was addressed: tax collectors and sinners were members of God's people. Likewise, both coin and son "belonged" to their respective households.

30

Luke 16:19–31. "Dives," Lazarus, & the Beatitudes

Goal

To show yet another instance where Luke unrelentingly pursues his redactional agenda, in this case by displaying another instance of L material alongside modified Q. We also see here (and elsewhere in Luke and the other Gospels) a different Christology and understanding of salvation than, say, would be promoted by St. Paul and many of his subsequent interpreters.

Beatitudes (Luke 6)	**"Dives" (L)**	**Lazarus (L)**
1. "Blessed are you [disciples] who are poor (20a)		poor (20), dogs licked sores (21)
2. for yours is the kingdom of God." (20b)		angels take to Abraham's side (22)
3. "Blessed are you who are hungry now,		hungry, desired crumbs (21)
for you will be filled" (21)		
4. "But woe to you who are rich, for	rich (19), tormented in Hades (23)	received "evil things" (25)
5. you have received your consolation" (24)	during his lifetime (25)	comforted (25)
[παρακαλεῖν]	received good things	[παρακαλεῖν]
6. "Woe to you who are full now,	feasted sumptuously daily (19)	
7.	you received your good things (25)	
8. for you will be hungry" (25)	place of agony (25), torment (28)	separated by a permanent chasm (26)

1. This is yet another example of a theme prominent in the material found in Luke alone. This is not to say that the other Evangelists lack such an emphasis. Rather, it is the case that Luke by his frequency hammers the point home.

2. Christian tradition since the late Middle Ages has given the anonymous rich man the name of "Dives," from the Latin meaning "rich," "a rich man."

3. Jesus cites Moses and the Prophets twice (vv. 29, 31). What does this suggest about their being sufficient to avoid torment in Hades? Is attention to those in such need merely a matter of ethics?

4. Of the many texts that could be cited, these samples are especially parallel to the Dives-Lazarus situation—where rich and poor are in proximity. The ideal is announced in the Fifth Book of Moses (Deut 15:11): "Open your hands to the poor and needy neighbor in your land." Revival and renewal are promised by the prophet Isaiah (58:6) if the fast of Yahweh's choosing is celebrated: "Is it not to share your bread with the hungry, and bring the homeless into your house?" Amos regards it as a transgression and sin to "push aside the needy in the gates" (5:12, the same Greek word for gate being used in the LXX and at Luke 16:20). Luke might also have cited the Writings (the third major division of the Hebrew Scriptures, sometimes designated as "Psalms"). According to Prov 28:7, "Whoever gives to the poor will lack nothing, but one who turns a blind eye will get many a curse." Job ups the ante even higher: "If I have withheld anything that the poor desired . . . or have eaten my morsel alone, . . . then let my shoulder blade fall from my shoulder and let my arm be broken from my socket. For I was in terror of calamity from God, and I could not have faced his majesty" (31:16–17, 22–23).

5. Does it come as a surprise that there is no explicit Christology here (or of a kind found elsewhere)—that it is through faith in Jesus alone (and by his atoning death) that one arrives at Abraham's side and avoids eternal torment? Is it enough that Jesus' authoritative word provides sufficient atonement? Several other prominent instances of such "salvation by the word of Jesus" appear in Luke's Gospel: the Lord's Prayer (11:1–4), the Parable of the Prodigal Father (15:11–32), the Parable of the Pharisee and Tax Collector (18:9–14), the Encounter

with Zaccheus (19:1–10). The last three appear only in L. One could also include instances of forgiveness by Jesus' spoken word (e.g., Luke 5:20–24 and synoptic parallels).

31

Luke 19:1–10 & 3:7–18. Zacchaeus & John the Baptizer

Goal

To demonstrate how, both earlier and later in his narrative, the Third Evangelist has employed L material to paint his portrait of Jesus and his mission. In the process, he shows how the Baptizer and Jesus are both similar and distinct. Human responsibility in the dynamics of being "saved" also comes to the fore.

John the Baptizer (3:7–18)	**Zacchaeus** (19:1–10)
1. Tax collectors come to John (12)	Chief tax collector, rich seeks Jesus (2)
2. Take no more than required. (13)	Fourfold restoration if fraud (8b)
3. Share clothes & food with the needy. (11)	Half of possessions to the poor (8a)
4. Repentance (8)	"salvation has come to this house" (9)
5. Preaching Good News (18)	
6. John the Messiah? (15)	"the Son of Man came to seek out and to save the lost" (10)

1. Here is an example of how Luke has employed L material to promote his emphasis on the relation between turning to God (l. 4) and attending to the needs of the poor (l. 3).
2. Matthew 3:8 (part of Q up to this point) also reports John's call to produce fruit matching ("worthy" = of equal value) repentance (l. 4). But Luke makes explicit what he means by that. See the display and analysis of 3:8–14 in Plot 6.

3. How do ll. 4 & 5 show that John and Jesus were not simply speaking of ethics?
4. That which John had generalized is specified in each case by the story of Zacchaeus. Traina, *Methodical Bible Study*, 51, 58 would cite this as an example of "particularization."
5. What is the potential significance of these two accounts appearing early and relatively late in the Gospel?
6. Can Jesus' role in salvation be confined to his death on the Cross? Would it not be more accurate (according to Luke's witness) to say, "Salvation is where Jesus is"?
7. From the larger context of this passage, how might "salvation" and "lost" be defined?
8. In ch. 3, the Baptizer sets the behavioral terms equivalent to repenting. Here, Jesus does not. Zacchaeus (not Jesus) himself articulates them as a function of the Son of Man's saving presence in his home.

32

Luke 19:45–46. Birds in Bezae (Codex D)[1]

Goal

Although each of the other Gospels (Matt 21:12–13//Mark 11:15–15//John 2:13–17) mentions doves and pigeons at this point in the narrative about Jesus' "cleansing" of the temple, only C. Bezae does so in Luke. This exercise seeks to explore the copyist's possible intent as an interpreter of the tradition.

Lev 12:1–8 (esp. v. 8)	Luke 2:22–24 (L)	Luke 19:45–46
1. Circumcision of Israelite poor[2]	Circumcision of Jesus	"Cleansing" by Jesus
2. Door to the Tent of Meeting	Temple	Temple
3. Pigeons	Pigeons	Pigeons
4. Turtledoves	Turtledoves	Turtledoves
5.		Den of thieves

1. One could accuse the scribe of trying to harmonize Luke's account with that of the other three Gospels. However, what else has he done since the author had included L material at 2:22–24? Whom might he have been attempting to identify, both as the "class" from among whom Jesus originated and the subject of the temple traders' exploitation?

1. The full name of this (late fourth? early fifth c.?) manuscript is "Codex Bezae Cantabrigiensis" because the French Protestant theologian Theodore Beza presented it to the University of Cambridge in the sixteenth century.

2. Another instance where these birds are acceptable offerings by the poor is found in Lev 14:22.

2. Such "interpolations" indicate that copyists were interpreters of tradition as well as its preservers. Of course, there is at least a possibility that this was the original reading; but scholars generally choose the shorter and less specific textual variant—tendencies to lengthen and embellish increasing over time.

3. It needs to be remembered that, now studied as a *manuscript* by academics at a university, this had in fact been an actual *Bible* preached and taught in an ecclesial setting. Before becoming the stock-in-trade of scholars, it had been the province of churchmen. Prior to laying the foundation (along with C. Sinaiticus, Vaticanus, and Alexandrinus) for the critical reconstruction of the GNT, it had been employed for worship and theological reflection. In advance of its being housed in a research library for access to specialists and (now, via the Internet[3]) by the general public, it had nurtured the life of congregations and perhaps a monastic community. Before being revered for its antiquity and quality, it had enjoyed a level of canonical authority. We must take with utmost seriousness the fact that, originally, the home of all codices had been the ancient church (as "pulpit Bibles"?) rather than the modern academy (as "desk copies").

3. See "Codex Bezae."

33

Luke 21:5–34 & Isaiah 13. The Destruction of Jerusalem

The Shaking of the Foundations

Goal

Although all three SG (TT) present a version of the "Little Apocalypse," the goal here is to interpret Luke's edition of in light of prophetic, biblical categories rather than by modern literalistic, historicistic, and rationalistic ones.

	ISAIAH 13[1]	LUKE 21:5–34
1. City/Empire	Babylon (1)	Jerusalem, temple (5–6, 20–21)
2. Occasion	Day of Lord (6, 9)	"days of vengeance" (22), "great distress on the earth," "wrath against this people" (23), Son of Man coming in a cloud with power and great glory" (27) "that day" (34)
3. Political upheaval	kingdoms, nations gathering (4)	wars & insurrections (9), nation vs. nation, kingdom vs. kingdom (10), kingdom of God near (31)
4. Human Suffering	Pangs, agony, anguish—as a woman in labor (8)	Dreadful for pregnant & nursing women (23)

1. According to the LXX, the translation most cited by NT authors.

	ISAIAH 13[1]	LUKE 21:5–34
5. Cosmic disruption	*sun dark . . . moon not shed light* *stars not give light* (10) *heaven will be enraged* (13), *and earth will be quaked*	*signs sun, moon* *stars* (25) *powers of the heavens will be shaken* (26) *great earthquakes* (11)
6. Earthly agents	Medes (17)	Gentile armies → captive (24)
7. City/Empire	Babylon (19)	Jerusalem, Judea (20–21)

1. Note that Isaiah 13 speaks of a historical event: the destruction of Babylon by the Medes (1, 17, 19). Did the cosmic disruption (vv. 10–13) actually occur on this occasion? If not, is this a dramatic way of saying that the destruction is to be thorough, that Babylon does not stand a chance, that "heaven itself" will fight against it? In Deborah's "sung" version of Sisera's defeat (Judges 4), the stars are said to have fought from their orbits in the sky against him (5:20).
2. If this is so for Isaiah 13 in the OT, might it not also be the case for Luke 21 in the NT? Did the phenomena of (vv. 11, 25–26) occur when Jerusalem was destroyed in 70 CE? Do we insist that they must occur in the future? Is this a special kind of biblical-prophetic language to speak of earthly, historical events? See especially Caird, "Language of Eschatology," 243–71.
3. These questions are even more pertinent for Luke than for Matthew and Mark, since he alone (L) emphasizes the surrounding of Jerusalem by Gentile armies, the prohibition against entering the city, and the taking captive of those not slain by the sword (vv. 20–24). Such historical references are entirely in keeping with Luke's exclusive citing (more L) of imperial and regional political rulers and religious officials during the birth of Jesus (2:1–2) and the ministry of John the Baptizer (3:1–2).
4. It is important to interpret v. 27 in the light of Dan 7:13–14. First, is there anything in Luke 21 that demands a *downward* movement of the Son of Man? What is the direction in Daniel? Continue asking the question, "What did Daniel and Jesus see? Was it a direct perception of reality or did they envision a mediating set of symbols?"

5. Pointing to an increase of catastrophic, natural phenomena as "signs of the times" is risky business. In North America, hurricanes generally occur on the East Coast, tornadoes in the Midwest (down "Tornado Alley"), and earthquakes on the West Coast (which belongs to the "Ring of Fire" circling the Pacific Ocean in both hemispheres). A similar geological phenomenon has disrupted the Mediterranean Basin. A 24/7 news cycle sometimes gives the impression that such occurrences are taking place more frequently.

34

Luke 22:15, 20. What Kind of Sacrifice?

(Exodus 12, 24, & Leviticus 16)

Goal

To identify more precisely the nature of Jesus' death, according to Luke, since he is sometimes said to lack or minimize a certain kind of atonement theology.

	PASSOVER (Exodus 12)	SINAI COVENANT (Exod 24:1–8) (see Jer 31:31–34)	***DAY OF ATONEMENT*** *(Leviticus 16)*
Animal Sacrifice	lamb(s)	ox(en)	*2 goats* *—slain* *—freed ("scapegoat")*
Purpose/Result	protection → liberation of the **community** from Egyptian slavery	sealing/bonding of the **community**	*release from the* ***community's*** *sins by the* ***live*** *animal*
Date/Time	spring	no annual observance	*late summer or early fall*

1. The blood sacrifices of three different animals achieved different results at different times of the year.
2. Sacrifices were for those who were *already* God's people, called by him into special relationship as early as Genesis 12. They were not initiatory rites.

3. The Passover Sacrifice was not for the forgiveness of sins, nor was Covenant Bonding. The former celebrated the community's freedom from Egypt so that Israel as a people could be joined by covenant to God.

4. Sacrifices on the Day of Atonement did not *get* Israelites "saved"; they *kept* them "saved"—salvation not understood as going to heaven and avoiding hell. Note that penalties for breaking the Ten Commandments (and all other injunctions of the Covenant) were entirely earth-bound.

5. Jesus did not die on the Day of Atonement (which was almost 6 months separate from Passover). And Passover was not an occasion for achieving forgiveness. Rather, it celebrated protection from the Angel sent throughout Egypt to kill all firstborn males, excepting those whose parents had spread the lamb's blood on their doorposts (Exodus 12). This led to Pharaoh's releasing the Israelites from slavery.

6. Only the first two columns, "Passover" and "Covenant," are relevant to the Last Supper accounts, including Luke's. Is it then legitimate to infer that the Lukan Jesus viewed his death as achieving liberation and covenant bonding? See the special attention given to the Plot 35 for Luke 22:20.

35

Luke 22:20. The Blood of the New Covenant

Goal

To understand Luke's version of Jesus' words of institution over the cup in light of the other SG and in view of the only other covenant instituted with blood. This is especially needful, given the rarity with which Jesus speaks about the meaning and significance of his death.

	Original Covenant (Exod 24:1–7)	**"my blood of the covenant"** (Mark 14:24//Matt 26:28)	**"the new covenant in my blood"** (Luke 22:20)
Priest	Moses	Jesus	Jesus
Sacrificial Victim(s)	oxen	Jesus	Jesus
Bonding (scope)	God & Israel	God, 12 Disciples, & Others	God, 12 Disciples, & Others

1. It is rare enough for Jesus to speak about his death, especially in public. Rarer still are attempts to explain its nature, even to his own students in private. Exodus 24 is the only place where "covenant" and "blood" appear together, half of the latter thrown by Moses against the altar, the other half sprinkled over the newly liberated people of Israel. So, this is the one to which Jesus refers when he speaks of a particular ("the") covenant. Matthew alone adds that it was for the forgiveness of sins, a result associated with the Day of Atonement (Leviticus 16).
2. One should put "new" in brackets before the Matthean and Markan statements because the "better" manuscripts do not have the word.

Editors suspect that scribes wanted to harmonize the accounts (including Luke's and St. Paul's in 1 Cor 11:25) across the board.

This would also fit with the New Covenant of Jeremiah 31:31–33, which the Author of Hebrews cites and expounds (9:20). However, no blood sacrifice is mentioned in Jeremiah 31.

3. Was explication and harmonization Luke's intent as well?
4. However, what was implicitly new about it, given the display above? Although the categories are the same, what is different?

36

Luke 22:17–20. The Last Supper's Menu

Goal

To interpret the unique textual tradition recounting the Last Supper in its own right and in relation to the other SG. This illustrates how varied are the Gospel accounts in view of the liturgical streamlining that has subsequently occurred.

Luke a 22:17–19a	Luke b 22:19b–20	Matthew 26:26–28	Mark 14:22–24
1. Cup #1 (17–18)	= Cup #1 (17–18)		
2. Bread (19a)	= Bread (19a)	Bread	Bread
3.	Cup (#2) "of the NC in my blood" (19b–20)	Cup	Cup

1. The "best" manuscripts[1] include the longer, more awkward account. Those copies that are usually longer are the shortest at this and other points.
2. Each of the two Lukan readings poses a difficulty: the first (the shorter: Luke a) contains a sequence reversed in the other Gospels. The second (the longer: Luke b) maintains the other's order; but it is still problematized by the earlier cup.

1. This is a relative category: the best reading is *usually* shorter, *usually* less specific, and *usually* problematic (either stylistically or theologically). These criteria for internal evidence are supplemented by criteria for external evidence: the age and distribution of manuscript support. The classic work on this subject is Metzger, *Text of the New Testament*. Its practice can be observed in Metzger, *A Textual Commentary*.

3. Who has been responsible for selecting from the diverse accounts of the *Last* Supper the version used in the liturgy of the *Lord's* Supper? The words of institution cited by St. Paul follow the sequence of Matthew and Mark (1 Cor 11:23–26). The FG contains no account of such a final meal.
4. Given the nature and state of the Gospels' evidence, how justified is it to insist on a particular sequence and elements, thereby being a source of division within the church over this rite?

37

Luke 22:27–30. Status and Role in the Kingdom of God

Goal

To elucidate further the particular flavor of Luke's Last Supper scene, which differs in important details from the other SG. Noticing how Luke goes about adopting, adapting, and arranging his material enlarges one's understanding of power and leadership in the community of Jesus' students/learners.

ll.	Matthew 20:28	Mark 10:45	Luke 22:27–30
1			[27] "'For who is greater, the one who
2			is at table, or the one who serves? Is it
3			not the one at the table?
4	". . . 'just as the Son of Man came not to	"'For the Son of Man came not to	But I am among you as one
5	be served but to serve, and to give his	be served but to serve, and to give his	who serves.
6	life a ransom for many.'"	life a ransom for many.'"	
7			[28]You are those who have stood by me
8	**Matthew 19:28**		in my trials; [29]and I confer on you, just as
9	"'Truly I tell you, at the renewal of all		
10	things, when the Son of Man is seated on		
11	the throne of his glory, you who have		my Father conferred on me, a kingdom, so

II.	Matthew 20:28	Mark 10:45	Luke 22:27–30
12	followed me will also		[30] that you may eat and drink at my table in
13			my kingdom, and you will
14	sit on twelve thrones, judging		sit on thrones judging
15	the twelve tribes of Israel.'"		the twelve tribes of Israel.'"

1. Each of the SG records two instances where disciples (named in Matthew and Mark) desire high(er) rank and status among themselves, requiring Jesus to teach them about true greatness, citing his own example as the Son of Man.[1] What do you infer about his having to make this point twice?
2. The first two Evangelists position both accounts earlier in their Gospels, immediately following the second and third Passion Predications about the Son of Man's suffering, death, and resurrection.[2] Readers have naturally balked at how insensitive their request was in the light of them.
3. Like the others, Luke places the first teaching about status and role after the second Passion Prediction (9:44); but he alone puts the second such instruction in the context of the Last Supper (22:24–30). What is signified by such a shift?
4. Luke alone associates this and the previous discourse (Plot 36, vv. 16 and 18) with kings and kingdoms (twice earlier and three times here). What does such frequency in close proximity suggest regarding earlier preaching and teaching about God's Rule?
5. The Third Evangelist also forwards the Q statement about judging the twelve tribes of Israel into this context, the royal and judicial roles combined in the role of the Ancient of Days in Daniel 7, which is presumably then bequeathed to the authorized, glorified, and enthroned son of man figure (vv. 9–14).
6. The theo- or patri-centric nature of Jesus' teaching is seen here yet again: he bequeaths the kingdom to his disciples, the kingdom that has been

1. Matt 18:1–5, 20:20–28; Mark 9:33–37, 10:42–45; Luke 9:46–47, 22:24–30.
2. Matt 17:22–23, 20:18–19; Mark 9:31, 10:33–34.

handed over to him by his Father. The reverse direction of this derived relationship is also reflected across the Gospel tradition in various permutations: the one who receives (δέχεσθαι) the disciples, receives Jesus; and the one receiving Jesus, receives the one who sent him.[3]

7. What is the force of Luke's switching from third person references to the Son of Man's acting as servant (in an overall statement of purpose) to the first person singular (in this particular context)?
8. Jesus "knows his place" at the Table. How does this fit with the reversal theme that has been prominent since chapter 1?

3. Matt 10:40, Mark 9:37, Luke 10:16, John 13:20. Mark's version is the most stark: "Whoever welcomes [δέχεσθαι] one such child in my name welcomes me; and whoever welcomes me welcomes not me but the one who sent me." See also the comparatively stunning statement in John 12:44.

38

Luke 23:35–47. At the Crucifixion: Luke & the Wisdom of Solomon.

A Paradigm Regained

Goal

To illustrate how the LXX's Deuterocanon provides a context for understanding the differences among the SG (TT) accounts of statements made at the crucifixion (climaxing in the centurion's "confession," which differs so much from that in Matthew and Mark). Even those who reject this document's canonical status can agree that the Gospels should be read within the religious and literary environment of Second Temple Judaism.

	Wis Sol 2:12–20	Luke 23:35–47	Mark 15:27–39 //Matt 27:38–54
1. Who? (subject/ source)	unknown figure	Jesus	ditto
2. What? (event)	ridicule at abusive event	ridicule at crucifixion	ditto
3. for Whom? (object)	[Jewish readers]	[Gentile Christian readers]	[ditto//Jewish-Christian readers]
4. against Whom? (object)	"***righteous*** (or ***just***) **man**	**"This man was *innocent*"**	**"Truly this man was**
	is *God's son*"	(or ***just***, or ***righteous***)."	**God's Son**."
	[ὁ δίκαιος υἱὸς θεοῦ]	[δίκαιος]	[υἱὸς θεοῦ]
	(18)	(47)	(Mark 15:39//Matt 27:54)

	Wis Sol 2:12–20	Luke 23:35–47	Mark 15:27–39 //Matt 27:38–54
5. by Whom? (agent)	hedonist, lawless ungodly	Gentile Roman centurion	ditto
6. Why? (reason/ cause)	threat to way of life	threat: religious & political	ditto
7. How? (means)	verbal & physical attack	condemnation by authorities	ditto
8. Result	insult, torture, death intended	death	ditto
9. So what? (significance)	a known paradigm	known paradigm embodied	ditto
10. When? (time)	unspecified	Passover	ditto
11. Where? (place)	unspecified	Jerusalem—Calvary	ditto

1. For 2000 years, the Wisdom of Solomon, along with other deutero-canoncal writings, has been integrated in Bibles of the Roman Catholic and Eastern Orthodox Churches (including the Coptic and Ethiopian). Protestant reformers in the sixteenth century broke with this tradition by segregating these books between the OT protocanonical writings of the HB and the books of the NT, labeling the former with the pejorative connotation, "Apocrypha" (lit. "hidden things"). From this point on among Protestant denominations, they functioned at best as historical resources for the "intertestamental" period (roughly four centuries) and as non-binding guides to pious living, but not for doctrine. Early in the nineteenth century, Protestant publishers excluded them altogether. When ecumenical winds started blowing in the 1960s, versions of the Bible containing the Deuterocanon began being made generally accessible for a Protestant readership—as in the case of the RSV, NEB, and now NRSV.
2. One of the values of relating the Wisdom of Solomon to this scene in the Gospels is that it may help to explain why Luke and the other synoptics differ at the point of the centurion's confession (l. 4): the "righteous/ just/innocent [δίκαιος] person" and "son of God" belonged within the same theological environment, being virtual equivalents. The Third

Evangelist chose one of them, and the others the alternative. Thus, Luke's is neither lesser nor more historical. Nor did the other Gospel writers necessarily choose the greater or less historical of the two.

3. The motif of a pious figure—who suffers such physical abuse and scorn—chronologically preceded the SG accounts (both historically and literarily within the LXX), linking the verbal abuse at Jesus' crucifixion with the phenomenon of reproach against God's agent. In the SG, Jesus is faced with the contradiction that, as God's messiah/ Christ, he ought to count on divine aid (or save himself—just as he had others).

4. In the Wisdom of Solomon 2, the figure is charged with calling himself "'a child [OSB] of the Lord' or 'servant of the Lord'" (13) (παῖς, not δοῦλος) and is accused of calling God his Father (16). Only in the Garden of Gethsemane, just before his arrest, does Jesus address God in this manner (14:36). According to the other two SG, the only other place where Jesus does so is at Luke 10:22//Matt 11:27.

5. With great irony, Mark and Matthew render this *accusation* by the leaders of Jesus' own people as an *affirmation* by the Gentile executioner.

6. Immediately preceding this section is Jesus' stunning pronouncement forgiving his executioners (v. 34): "but Jesus was saying [the Greek suggesting continuous action], 'Father, forgive them, for they do not know what they are doing'" (translation mine). Because early manuscripts are unevenly divided over its inclusion, critical texts and modern translations either bracket the statement or subsume it in a footnote.[1] Its presence corresponds with other instances in the SG where Jesus pronounces forgiveness without reference to his death, per se (although he is at that moment on the cross). Do we have here yet another example of Luke's more comprehensive soteriology: salvation is where Jesus is, and can come by what he says?

7. Imbedded within this section is Luke's much-expanded account about the two evildoers crucified alongside Jesus (vv. 39–43). Matthew and Mark devote but a single sentence to their deriding him.[2] What is significant about that which follows? The Third Evangelist alone records one of them blaspheming Jesus. The other—acknowledging his

1. See Metzger, *Textual Commentary*, 180 for a full discussion.

2. The are identified as "thieves" or "brigands" (λῃσταί) in Matthew & Luke.

deserved punishment—asks to be remembered when he comes into his kingdom. Where is the expected, conditional language of repentance or belief? Does Jesus pronounce forgiveness? Rather, he says, "Truly I tell you, today you will be with me in Paradise" (v. 43). Here is a robust, dynamic atonement—minus the language of the cult. And so Jesus died as he had lived: "numbered among transgressors" (Isa 53:12).

39

Luke 24:36–43. The Resurrection Body

(With All Due Respect to St. John)

Goal

Although the FG makes the stunning assertion that "the Word became flesh" (1:14), it is Luke who narrates the extent of that embodiment, as the following display and discussion show.

Luke	John
1.	to Mary: "stop holding on to me"[1] (20:17).
2. to disciples: "'Look at my hands and my feet.'" "Touch me and see;	to Thomas: "'Put your finger here and see my hands.
3. . . . for a ghost does not have flesh and bones" (24:39).	Reach out your hand and put it in my side'" (20:27).
4.	to disciples: "'Come and have breakfast'" (21:12).
5. to Cleopas & friend: "he took bread . . . and gave it to them" (24:30).	for disciples: Jesus served bread and fish (v. 13).
6. Jesus: "'Have you anything here to eat?'" (24:40).	

1. The present imperative with the negative in Greek is used to terminate an activity already in progress. Translations along the lines of "Do not touch me" may be used, without warrant, to suggest that there was something inappropriate for Jesus to have been touched (particularly by a woman).

Luke	John
7. "They gave him a piece of broiled fish" (v. 42).	
8. and he took it and ate in their presence" (v. 43).	

1. Both Luke and John underscore the tangible nature of Jesus' post-resurrection body (ll. 2 & 3).
2. While it's possible to infer that Jesus, according to John, joined his disciples in eating the meal that he had provided (ll. 4–5), Luke leaves no doubt about it (ll. 6–8). He reinforces this point at Acts 10:41. The apostles, as witnesses, "'ate and drank with him after he rose from the dead.'" Of course, Jesus had participated in the Passover meal before his death, identifying the event in his own words (unique to the Third Evangelist): "'I have eagerly desired to eat this Passover with you before I suffer'" (22:15). Twice (again uniquely), he looks forward to resuming that activity in the kingdom of God (vv. 16 & 18).[2]
3. In their different ways, each of the Gospel writers seems to be countering dualistic tendencies (gnostic, docetic, etc.) that deny a positive view of the body and its compatibility with (and indispensability for) the life of the spirit and mind. Would it be fair to conclude that Luke goes the farthest among them? For a treatment of St. John's imagery of consuming the Son of Man's flesh and blood (6:40–68), see Lemcio, *Soaring*, 34–45 and 57–58.

2. Marshall, *Last Supper and Lord's Supper*, 180–81 (Table 2) conveniently sets forth the SG's accounts alongside that of St. Paul's in 1 Cor 11:23–25. Table 1 (p. 179) displays the elements of the Passover Feast during four days of celebration.

40

Luke 24:46–47 & 4:18–19. Jubilary Forgiveness & Release

One Kerygma or Two? Apples & Oranges?

Goal

To determine whether or not there is a pre-Easter kerygma or gospel in Luke 4 that differs from a post-Easter kerygma in Luke 24.

1. Was Jesus' pre-Easter messianic mission to proclaim (κηρύξαι) release (ἄφεσιν) to the captives and "to let the oppressed go free" (ἐν ἀφέσει) (4:18), whereas the post-Easter mission of the disciples—"repentance for the forgiveness [ἄφεσιν] of sins—was to be proclaimed [κηρυχθῆναι] in [the Christ's] name to all the nations" (24:47)? In other words, do we have here the annunciation of two kerygmata: one appropriate during Jesus' life and the other suitable for the church's life after his death and resurrection?
2. The contrast is in part a function of how one should convey the sense of ἄφεσις, which appears in both passages. It's the usual word for "release" or "let go." Most translations into European languages render the instance in Luke 4 as "release" and the second one in chapter 24 as "forgiveness," a word whose meaning is not simply the sum of "for" and "give." However, two translations of which I am aware render ἄφεσις in both chapters as "release."[1]
3. The possibility that this might be a distinction without a fundamental difference is suggested by the LXX of Isaiah 61, which Luke's Jesus

1. See the Polish "odpuszczenie," *Nowy Testament z Ilustracijami*. The "Kulish Bible," the first full translation in the modern era into Ukrainian, has "vidpushchennyu," *S'vyate Pys'mo*. However, its successor, the "Ohienko Bible," also published by the BFBS (now by the Ukrainian Bible Society in Kyiv), has the equivalent of "forgiveness" at this point.

quotes in chapter 4. The end of the citation, "the acceptable year c the Lord" (v. 18) seems to allude to the Year of Jubilee in Leviticus 25, rendered in the LXX as ἔτος ἀφέσεως ("Year of Release"). In fact, that chapter is full of "release" language.

4. Rarely noted is that the Year of Release begins on the Day of Atonement (ἡμέρα ἱλασμοῦ) (Lev 25:9), when the High Priest (originally Aaron) will release (ἀφήσει) a live goat, bearing away Israel's sins into the desert (Lev 16:10. Cf. 21–22). There then follows a series of actions: liberating people from debts, letting them go from servitude incurred by debts, releasing the land from production, and freeing the land from perpetual ownership. God is the land's Lord; the people are tenants on it (vv. 10–55).

5. I propose that the Year of Release in Leviticus 25 is the backdrop for the announcement of forgiveness/release (ἄφεσις) in chapter 24 and release (ἄφεσις) in chapter 4. More specifically, the mission attributed to Jesus' proclamation (κηρύσσειν, εὐαγγελίζεσθαι) of release in chapter 4 presupposes the forgiveness/release of sins on the Day of Atonement (Lev 25:9), when the Year of Jubilee/Release begins. In chapter 24, the forgiveness/release (ἄφεσις) of sins that Jesus' followers are to proclaim (κηρύσσειν) among all the nations presupposes the liberation of all that enslaves (Lev 25:10–55[2]). Luke's second volume seems to bear this out in the early church's proclamation of forgiveness, which leads to the Jubilary sharing of goods in Acts 2:43–47 and 4:32–37. The data are displayed as follows:

Leviticus 25	Luke 4:18–19	Luke 24:46–47	Acts 2
1. God of Israel (via Moses)	Jesus	Jesus' Commission	Peter
2.	Messianic [χρίειν] (Spirit-anointed) Mission	Messiah [Χριστός]	Messiah [Χριστός]
		—suffer & rise	—crucified → Lord (36)
3. Proclaim: διαγγέλειν (9)	—proclamation (3x): κηρύσσειν	κηρύσσειν	

2. This section is replete with the language of redemption (λυτρο–) that results in freedom or release.

Leviticus 25	Luke 4:18–19	Luke 24:46–47	Acts 2
4.	—announcing Good News: εὐαγγελίζεσθαι		διαμαρτυρεῖν (40)
5. Atonement: redemption			
6. Release: ἔτος ἀφέσεως	Release: ἄφεσις (2x: 18)	forgiveness: ἄφεσις	forgiveness (38): ἄφεσιν
7. -slaves, land, debts (10–55)	-captives, oppressed		Needs met (43–47, 4:32–37)
8. -of Israelites	-of Jews → Gentiles/ nations	-to all nations	-of Jewish believers
9. -every 50 years	-today	-always	-Pentecost and after
10. -Israel	-Nazareth synagogue → beyond Israel	-from Jerusalem	-in Jerusalem

6. In other words, could we say that LXX Leviticus 25 provides the backdrop of the kerygmata preached in both Luke 4 and 24? Just as Luke 4 presupposes the atonement element of Lev 25:9, so Luke 24 presupposes the community ethics element of Lev 25:10–55.
7. Otherwise, we would have to argue that Luke meant to differentiate between the content and idiom of Jesus' and the church's gospel proclamation (as he did for other christological and theological categories). I took this position in *Past of Jesus*, 13–15, 74–90. My thesis was that each of the Gospel writers distinguishes between his own time and that of Jesus' era—contrary to the prevailing scholarly consensus that the Evangelists overlaid their accounts of his past with their own present, post-Easter theological agendas.

41

Savior Gods in the Mediterranean World[1]

Goal

To demonstrate that the Gospels contain terms and categories familiar to readers in the ancient world (and to those who since then have been knowledgeable about that era). Even more important is to demonstrate that, at least in one instance, a complete, similar pattern exists similar to that in both Luke and Matthew—not just fragments of the whole requiring some (or much!) assembly—minus instructions.

Readers who encounter such "parallels" to the Gospels in Greco-Roman accounts (myths) of heroes or demi-gods are often faced with two extreme alternative responses: (1) the parallels could not exist because, as monotheistic Jews, the earliest Christians would have rejected such borrowing of terms and patterns or (2) the parallels are evidence that Christians freely borrowed language and forms from their pagan neighbors in an attempt to reach them with the "true" version of such stories. The following comprehensive display sets forth the data so as to determine which lies nearer the truth or whether a third alternative accounts for the evidence best. Included in the statements that follow are bibliography whose authors incline towards the alternative's suggestions.

1. I have borrowed this title from an essay found in Cartlidge & Dungan, "Savior Gods," 13–22. My display summarizes, organizes, and labels the contents of this study and that by Young, "Two Roots," 87–121. Only ancient authors whose works clearly predate the Gospels' composition have been used. Not all of the categories that I have distinguished are represented in each case. However, the greatest number of them (represented by A–K) occurs in the account of Herakles (aka "Hercules") by Diodorus Siculus (*Library of History,* books II.35–IV.58 and IV.9.1–IV.39.4), whose myth presented the greatest challenge to early Christian apologists. See Plot 42 for a full analysis.

A Figure	B Pre-Existence	C Genealogy	D Divine Father	E Human "Father"	F Human Mother	G Conception
1. Ptolemy V Rosetta Stone (196 BCE)		Child of the Gods				
2. Epicurus Lucretius (94–55 BCE)						
3. HERAKLES Diod. Sic. (1st c. BCE)		**Zeus (both sides)**	**Zeus**	**Amphy-trion**	**Alkmene**	**By deceit**
4. "The Boy" Virgil, 4th Eclog. (44 BCE)	New offspring Heaven-sent	Beloved offspring of the gods				
5. Romulus Ovid (3 BCE)						

H Names	I Deeds/Words	J Violent Death	K Aftermath / Appearances
1. Living Image of Zeus Priest of Gods God Visible			
2. He was a god	Philosopher/revealer Brought solace to minds Philosophy = euangelion		
3. (Adopted son of Hera)	**12 Deeds, infidelities** **Wars over lovers**	**Enemy's poison** **Self-cremation**	**Translation to "heaven"** **Declines "Immortal" offer** **Worshiped as god**
4.	Erase vestiges of wickedness Release earth from dread Rule world made peaceful by Father		
5.			Taken up by Mars —Mortal body dissolved —Gets beautiful form Reappears w. commission —"Cultivate war" Returns

A Figure	B Pre-Existence	C Genealogy	D Divine Father	E Human "Father"	F Human Mother	G Conception
6. "The Boy" Livy (25 BCE)						
7. Augustus Asia Minor Assembly (9 BCE)			Providence			Birthday
8. Augustus Horace (30 BCE)	Immortal shape	Mercury				Take mortal shape Descend
9. Caligula[2] Ephesian Council (48 CE)		Ares Aphrodite				

2. This is the only entry not securely earlier than the gospels. However, I include it as a contemporaneous example.

H Names	I Deeds/Words	J Violent Death	K Aftermath / Appearances
6. Declared a god,		Senators assassinate	Ascends by a storm cloud
the Son of God[3] (see 6.K)			Descends:
			—"Cultivate military"
			Returns (see 6.H)
7. Birthday as god	Filled w. virtue for human		
—celebrated	welfare: peace, order		
Savior, the God	Surpassed all benefactors		
	Gospel		
8. Prince, Father	Prop up Rome		Return to skies
	Atone		
9. High Priest,			
Absolute Ruler			
God visible			
Savior			

3. For a recent assessment of the title in Jewish, Greco-Roman, and Christian contexts, see Broad, *Alexander or Jesus?*

1. Although one might with justification conclude that no such figure as Herakles had ever existed (and that individual differences are significant, especially at the moral level), the striking parallels in the *overall pattern* need to be addressed. I provide them because such ancient stories have been all but obliterated from school curricula. However, that there is something of a comeback occurring is evidenced by books for children, some of which have been awarded the highest honors for this genre. See the Bibliography under D'Aulaire and D'Aulaire, *Book of Greek Myths*; Lipson et al., *Mighty Myth*; McCaughrean, *Hercules*; and McDermott, *Arrow to the Sun* (a Navajo tale that received the Caldecott Medal Award for Illustration). Then there is Disney's "cherry-picked" and "air-brushed" animated film *Hercules* (1997).

2. I have emboldened category 3, as the account of Heracles contains almost all of the elements found in the Gospels of Luke and Matthew. The Fourth Gospel, though starting with the beginning of the Word, reports neither genealogy nor birth-infancy stories.

3. See the comparisons and contrasts with the Gospels in Plot 42: "A Common Narrative Pattern: Herakles/Hercules & Jesus in the Gospels."

4. For a modern attempt, even from within conservative Christian circles, to embrace myth positively, see Fuller et al., *Myth, Allegory, and Gospel*; Lewis, *The Lion, the Witch and the Wardrobe*, and "Myth Became Fact"; Lockerbie, *Liberating Word*; and Markos, "Myth Matters."

42

A Common Narrative Pattern

Herakles/Hercules & Jesus in the Gospels[1]

Goal

As the display below illustrates, Luke and Matthew share with the biography of Herakles/Hercules the following elements of a narrative pattern: (1) genealogy, (2) divine father, (3) human (adoptive) father, (4) human mother, (5) supernatural conception, (6) exalted names/status, (7) mighty deeds/words, (8) opposition, (9) violent death, (10) appearances/aftermath. As a result, it is important to clarify misconceptions of two kinds. The first is by well-meaning Christians who apply unsophisticated definitions of "myth" to any hint that the authors of the Bible (being strict monotheists) would have used the genre in any way to convey their convictions about the only true God of Israel and the church. The other is by comparative religionists of various hues, who make imprecise statements about the meaning of myth in general and about the nature of the biblical writers' appropriation of myth(s) in particular. (In other words, it is possible both to claim too much and also too little about the meaning and function of myth in Scripture.) Only by a close look at actual texts, both biblical and extra-biblical, can an accurate response to both extremes be formulated. These displays are intended to aid in that effort.

1. See note 1 of Plot 41 ("Savior Gods of the Mediterranean World"), where I cite the work of Diodorus Siculus (first c. BCE), who provides the most continuous, pre-Christian narrative of Herakles's life. Rather than assemble a composite account of this (or any other) hero's story, my aim has been to call attention to a comprehensive, extra-biblical *framework* or *template* that could be compared and contrasted with an intra-gospel *pattern*.

a prose summary of Herakles for those unfamiliar with it would be nice

		Jesus		
	Herakles	**Luke**	**Matthew**	**John**
1. Pre-existence	–0–	–0–	–0–	"In the beginning"
2. Genealogy	Those of both parents	Backwards to Adam	Forwards from Abraham	–0–
3. Divine Father	Zeus	God/Spirit	Same	–0–
4. Human (Adoptive) Father	Amphytrion	Joseph	Same	–0–
5. Human Mother	Alkmene	Mary	Same	–0–
6. Supernatural Conception	By deceit, sexual	Consensual, asexual	Same, virginal	–0–
7. Exalted Name(s)/ Status	Hera's adopted son	"Son of the Most High"	"Son of David & Abraham"	"Word," "Son"
		"Christ, the Lord"	"Messiah," "Emmanuel"	
8. Mighty Deeds/ Words	12 labors [πράξεις]	Healings	Same	Same [ἔργα]
	Illicit affairs	Exorcisms	Same	–0–
		Nature miracles	Same	Same
		Teachings	Same	Same
9. Opposition	Wars with husbands	Religious opposition	Same	Same
10. Violent Death	Poisoning by enemy	Crucifixion	Same	Same
	Immolation by friend			

		Jesus		
	Herakles	**Luke**	**Matthew**	**John**
11. Aftermath	Heavenly bolt consumes pyre → no bones, apotheosis	Bodily resurrection	Same	Same

1. The display shows that we are not simply dealing with "parallels" to this or that individual phase of Jesus' life (birth, life, death, or reappearance).[2] Rather, it is the entire narrative framework that should be comparable.
2. Thus, differences, even serious ones, between the Greco-Roman myths and those of the Gospel do not invalidate comparisons with the *categories* comprising the *pattern* common to them. This is why I have limited my example to continuous rather than fragmentary accounts.
3. The presence of similarities does not necessitate determining which account came first or who borrowed from whom. Rather, one can think of deeply embedded, shared cultural archetypes.
4. Lacking an infancy narrative, Mark's Gospel is omitted from the comparisons. The Second and Fourth Gospels, in which infancy narratives are absent, illustrate that Evangelists were not obliged to include them (on the assumption that such were available).
5. Although Alkmene (#5) was not a virgin, she was chaste. Zeus was able to seduce her (#6) only by deception: taking the form of her absent husband, Amphytrion.
6. A distinction is being made in #6 between the "fact" of divine conception and the manner of that conception. Luke (1:37) and Matthew (1:23) use παρθένος of Mary. See the study by Charles Isbell ("Mary's Virginity?"), who argues that even the Greek word in some contexts can refer more generally to an unmarried woman who is not necessarily a virgin.

2. C. H. Talbert concentrates on the beginning and end of the pattern, especially in Hellenistic-Jewish texts, in "Myth of the Descending-Ascending Redeemer." Andrew Lincoln focuses on Jesus' birth in *Born of a Virgin?*

7. Regarding #7: throughout the narrative, Jesus' own preferred term is "the Son of Man."

8. Christians who tried coming to terms with this predominantly heroic figure made much of the moral differences (#8) in the accounts of Herakles and those about Jesus. But pagans also found the moral issues problematic, despite efforts to allegorize Herakles's failures. See esp. the discussion by van Kooten, "Christianity in the Graeco-Roman World," esp. "The competition between Christ and Heracles," 25–29.

9. A lightning bolt from heaven (Zeus) consumes the pyre upon which Herakles had placed himself. A friend had reluctantly set fire to the "altar" (#10–11). Herakles declines joining the twelve Olympian gods, though Hera adopts him as her son. Compare and contrast with the Gospels' accounts

10. If one objects that the earliest Christians, as monotheistic Jews, would not have tolerated such appropriation, it should be remembered that Jews (even in Judea and Jerusalem) had been Hellenized in various degrees for over 300 years. Synagogues show signs of appreciation for classical themes that could be adapted to biblical narratives. That the myth of Herakles was known (and appropriated by Jews?) in Palestinian territory itself (specifically, in Hippos-Sussita [Aramaic for "horse"]—a city of the Decapolis) before the Common Era, see Segal and Eisenberg, "Hercules in Galilee," 50–51. The authors point out that across the Sea of Galilee ("cheek by jowl") lay Jewish Tiberias, home to the Sanhedrin (51).

11. In subsequent centuries, Christians were divided on the value of such comparisons. On the one hand, Justin Martyr (mid-second c. CE), while acknowledging the similarities, regarded them as derivative and distorted representations of God's plan that demons had stolen, distributing them among mythographers and poets (*Apology*, 1.21–23). On the other hand, because of such "parallels," pagans should not be critical of Christian claims at this point. The Gospel versions were authentic because their moral character (especially that of Jesus) was so much higher.[3] How is it then, asks Justin, that non-Christian Gentile

3. It ought to be obvious that contemporary Christian apologetics cannot take Justin's approach. Nor can modern apologists deny outright either the pattern or its individual components. Otherwise, why would those closest to the Gospel accounts feel the need to justify the Christian version? One does not become defensive unless such smoke

parents sacrificed to beings whose behavior, were it to be repeated by their children, would be regarded as scandalous?

12. See works by Tolkien, Fuller, and others who would endorse a version of Lewis's notion that myth had become fact in Jesus. While early Christian apologists had claimed the *moral* high ground in the Gospel accounts, Lewis claimed the *historical* high ground. However, he never went beyond the level of assertion—suggesting only that the Evangelists' narratives, because they had emerged so close to the original events, were more accessible to the historian than the primarily mythic versions.

13. Although Lewis suggested that God had given pagans good dreams (*Mere Christianity*, 39), many women might hold that some of them contained nightmares—assault (both personal and impersonal) or deception.

14. For a late twentieth-century debate about several of the issues from various perspectives, see Hick, *Myth of God Incarnate*; Green, *Truth of God Incarnate*; and Goulder, *Incarnation and Myth*.

indicates fire—or at least smoldering embers. See note 1 of Plot 41 ("Savior Gods of the Mediterranean World") for an important caution about the dating of such extra-biblical, Greco-Roman sources.

Appendix

Origen on the Gospels' Diversity

Scholars often point to Clement of Alexandria, who distinguished between the bodily (*somatika*) accounts of the SG and the spiritual (*pneumatika*) version of the FG. Less commonly cited are the words of Origen, his successor (ca. 184–253 CE), who went so far as to say,

> I do no condemn them if they sometimes dealt freely with things which to the eye of history happened differently, and changed them so as to subserve the mystical aims they had in view—speaking of something that happened in one place as if it had happened in another or of something that took place at one time as if it had taken place at another, and introducing into what was spoken in a certain way some changes of their own. Where possible, they intended to speak the truth both materially and spiritually; and where this was not possible, they chose to prefer the spiritual to the material. Spiritual truth was often preserved, as one might say, in material falsehood.[1]

Origen's statement illustrates several issues that are as relevant in the present climate as they were significant then: he

1. acknowledged differences in accounts of time and place.
2. came to these conclusions by rationally exercising the criterion of non-contradiction.
3. recognized that there is a means of seeing through "the eyes of history."
4. avoided preferential treatment, harmonization, and reduction to a principle.
5. distinguished between outer/material truth and inner/spiritual or (theological) truth.

1. Origen, "Commentary on John," X.4.

6. was open to regarding the former as "false."
7. credited the Evangelists with *attempting* to tell the truth at both levels.

Might this be instructive about defusing some of the controversies regarding the historicity of the Gospels? Origen might not have been correct in his evaluation (by which criteria would one judge?), but his position —on this subject, at least—was not regarded as beyond the pale by the early church.

Bibliography of Cited Works

Aland, Kurt, and Barbara Aland. *Synopsis Quattuor Evangeliorum*. Stuttgart: Württembergische Bibelanstalt, 1964.

Barfield, Owen. "Meaning and Myth." In *Poetic Diction: A Study in Meaning*, 77–92. Middletown, CT: Wesleyan University Press, 1973.

Barzun, Jacques. "Reasons to De-Test the Schools." *New York Times*, Oct 11, 1988.

Bauckham, Richard. *Jesus and the Eyewitnesses: The Gospels as Eyewitness Testimony*. Grand Rapids: Eerdmans, 2006.

Boyarin, Daniel. *The Jewish Gospels: The Story of the Jewish Christ*. New York: New Press, 2012.

Broad, W. E. L. *Alexander or Jesus? The Origin of the Title "Son of God."* Eugene, OR: Pickwick, 2015.

Burkett, Delbert. *The Son of Man Debate: A History and Evaluation*. SNTSMS 107. Cambridge: Cambridge University Press, 1999.

Burridge, Richard. *Four Gospels, One Jesus? A Symbolic Reading*. Grand Rapids: Eerdmans, 1994.

Caird, George B. *The Language and Imagery of the Bible*. Philadelphia: Westminster, 1980.

———. "The Language of Eschatology." In *The Language and Imagery of the Bible*, 219–42. Philadelphia: Westminster, 1980.

———. "The Language of Myth." In *The Language and Imagery of the Bible*, 243–71. Philadelphia: Westminster, 1980.

Cartlidge, David R., and David Dungan. "Savior Gods in the Mediterranean World." In *Documents for the Study of the Gospels*, edited by David R. Cartlidge and David Dungan, 13–22. Minneapolis: Fortress, 1980.

Charles, R. H., ed. *Apocrypha and Pseudepigrapha of the Old Testament*. Vol. 2. Oxford: Clarendon, 1913.

Charlesworth, James H. *The Old Testament Pseudepigrapha*. Vol. 2. New York: Doubleday, 1985.

"Codex Bezae (MS Nn.2.41)." University of Cambridge Digital Library. http://cudl.lib.cam.ac.uk/view/MS-NN-00002-00041.

Conzelmann, Hans. *The Theology of St. Luke*. New York: Harper, 1960.

Cranfield, C. E. B. *The Gospel According to Saint Mark*. Cambridge: Cambridge University Press, 1959.

D'Aulaire, Ingri, and Edgar D'Aulaire. *D'Aulaires' Book of Greek Myths*. Garden City, NY: Doubleday, 1962.

Diodorus Siculus. *The Library of History.* Translated by C. H. Oldfather. LCL. Cambridge, MA: Harvard University Press, 1939.

Dittenberger, Wilhelmus. *Orientis Graeci Inscriptiones Selectae.* Vol. 2. Unaltered printing of original Leipzig, 1905 ed. New York: Georg Olms, 1960.

The English Hexapla: Exhibiting the Six Important English Translations of the New Testament Scriptures. London: Samuel Bagster & Sons, 1841.

Farrer, Austin. *The Triple Victory: Christ's Temptations According to Saint Matthew* London: Faith, 1965.

Fitzmyer, Joseph. *The Gospel According to Luke I-IX.* AB 28; New York: Doubleday, 1981.

Flusser, David. "Blessed Are the Poor in Spirit." *IEJ* 10 (1960) 1–13.

Forward, Martin. "A Pilgrimage of Grace: The Journey Motif in Luke-Acts." In *A Man of Many Parts: Essays in Honor of John Westerdale Bowker on the Occasion of His Eightieth Birthday*, edited by Eugene E. Lemcio, 62–75. Eugene, OR: Pickwick, 2015.

Fuller, Edmund, et al. *Myth, Allegory, and Gospel: An Interpretation of J. R. R. Tolkien, C. S. Lewis, G. K. Chesterton, and Charles Williams.* Minneapolis: Bethany Fellowship, 1974.

Funk, Robert W., ed. *New Gospel Parallels.* Vol. 2. Philadelphia: Fortress, 1985.

Goulder, Michael, ed. *Incarnation and Myth: The Debate Continued.* Grand Rapids: Eerdmans, 1979.

Greek Gods Paradise. "88 Video Games Based on Greek Mythology." April 27, 2018. http://greekgodsparadise.com/2018/04/27/video-games-based-on-greek-mythology/.

Green, Joel B. *The Gospel of Luke.* New International Commentary on the New Testament. Grand Rapids: Eerdmans, 1997.

Green, Michael, ed. *The Truth of God Incarnate.* Grand Rapids: Eerdmans, 1977.

Harvey, Antony N. *Jesus and the Constraints of History.* London: Duckworth, 1982.

Harvey, Van A. *The Historian and the Believer: The Morality of Historical Knowledge and Christian Belief.* London: SCM, 1967.

Hick, John, ed. *The Myth of God Incarnate.* London: SCM, 1977.

Holladay, Carl. *Theios Aner in Hellenistic Judaism: A Critique of the Use of This Category in New Testament Christology.* SBLDS 40; Atlanta: SBL, 1977.

Howard, Thomas. "Myth: A Flight to Reality." In *The Christian Imagination: Essays on Literature and the Arts*, edited by Leland Ryken, 201–9. Grand Rapids: Baker, 1981.

Huxley, Aldous. *Texts and Pretexts: An Anthology with Commentaries.* New York: Harper, 1933.

Isbell, Charles D. "Does the Gospel of Matthew Proclaim Mary's Virginity?" *BAR* 3.2 (1977) 8–19.

Jansen, John Frederick. *Exercises in Interpreting Scripture.* Philadelphia: Geneva, 1968.

Justin Martyr. *Apology.* http://www.newadvent.org/fathers/0126.htm.

Kee, Howard Clark. *The New Testament in Context: Sources and Documents.* Englewood Cliffs, NJ: Prentice-Hall, 1984.

———. *The Origins of Christianity: Sources and Documents.* Englewood Cliffs, NJ: Prentice-Hall, 1973.

———, trans. "The Testament of Levi." In *The Old Testament Pseudepigrapha: Apocalyptic Literature and Testaments*, edited by J. H. Charlesworth, 778, 794–96. Garden City, NY: Doubleday, 1983.

Lemcio, Eugene E. "Daniel and the Three (Principally in the Old Greek): 'Historical' Signs of the Eschatological Son of Man and Saints of the Most High—A Paradigm for

Gospels Christology & Discipleship." In *A Man of Many Parts: Essays in Honor of John Westerdale Bowker on the Occasion of His Eightieth Birthday*, edited by Eugene E. Lemcio. 43–61. Eugene, OR: Pickwick, 2015.

———. "The Gospels and Canonical Criticism." *BTB* 11 (1981) 114–22.

———. *Navigating Revelation: Charts for the Voyage; A Pedagogical Aid*. Eugene, OR: Wipf & Stock, 2011.

———. "The Parables of the Great Supper and the Wedding Feast: History, Redaction, and Canon." *HBT* 8.1 (1986) 1–26.

———. *The Past of Jesus in the Gospels*. SNTSMS 68. Cambridge: Cambridge University Press, 1991.

———. "The Role of Nathan, King David's Immediate Heir, in Luke's Genealogy: Proposal and Prediction." *CATR* 8.2 (2019) 127–31.

———. *Soaring with St. John: Flight Paths of the Eagle; A Pedagogical Aid*. Eugene, OR: Wipf & Stock, 2013.

———. *Travels with St. Mark: GPS for the Journey; A Pedagogical Aid*. Eugene, OR: Wipf & Stock, 2012.

Levine, Amy-Jill. "The Many Faces of the Good Samaritan—Most Wrong." *BAR* 38.1 (2012) 24, 68.

Lewis, C. S. *The Lion, the Witch and the Wardrobe*. London: Geoffrey Bles, 1950.

———. *Mere Christianity*. London: Geoffrey Bles, 1952.

———. "Myth Became Fact." In *God in the Dock*, 63–67. Grand Rapids: Eerdmans, 1970.

Lincoln, Andrew T. *Born of a Virgin? Reconceiving Jesus in the Bible, Tradition, and Theology*. Grand Rapids: Eerdmans, 2013.

Lipson, Greta B., et al. *Mighty Myth: A Modern Interpretation of Greek Myths for the Classroom*. Lancaster, CA: Good Apple, 1982.

Lockerbie, D. Bruce. *The Liberating Word: Art and the Mystery of the Gospel*. Grand Rapids: Eerdmans, 1974.

———. "Myth and Christian Reality." In *The Liberating Word: Art and the Mystery of the Gospel*, 39–50. Grand Rapids: Eerdmans, 1974.

Markos, Louis A. "Myth Matters." *CT* (April 23, 2001) 32–39.

Marshall, I. Howard. *Last Supper and Lord's Supper*. Milton Keynes, UK: Paternoster, 1996.

McCaughrean, Geraldine. *Hercules*. Oxford: Oxford University Press, 2003.

McDermott, Gerald. *Arrow to the Sun*. New York: Viking, 1974.

Metzger, Bruce M. *A Textual Commentary on the Greek New Testament*. 2nd ed. Peabody, MA: Hendrickson, 2006.

———. *The Text of the New Testament: Its Transmission, Corruption, and Restoration*. 3rd ed. Oxford: Oxford University Press, 1992.

Milton, John. *Complete Poems and Major Prose*. Edited by Merritt Y. Hughes. Indianapolis: Odyssey, 1957.

Nowy Testament z Ilustracijami. Warszawa: Brytyjskie i Zagraniczne Towarzystwo Biblijne [Warsaw: British and Foreign Bible Society], 1978.

Origen. "Commentary on John." X.4. http://www.earlychristianwritings.com/text/origen-john10.html.

Parsons, Peter. *City of the Sharp-nosed Fish: Greek Lives in Roman Egypt*. London: Weidenfeld & Nicolson, 2007.

Patterson, Stephen J. "The Oxyrhynchus Papyri: The Remarkable Discovery You've Probably Never Heard Of." *BAR* 37.2 (2011) 60–68.

Ringe, Sharon H. "The Jubilee Proclamation in the Ministry and Teaching of Jesus: A Tradition-Critical Study in the Synoptic Gospels and Acts." PhD diss., Union Theological Seminary, 1981.

Roberts, Benjamin T. "Gospel to the Poor." *The Earnest Christian and the Golden Rule* 7:3 (1864) 69–73.

Sanders, E. P. *Paul and Palestinian Judaism*. Philadelphia: Fortress, 1977.

Sanders, James A. *God Has a Story Too: Sermons in Context*. Philadelphia: Fortress, 1979.

Sandmel, Samuel. "Parallelomania." *JBL* 81 (1962) 1–13.

Schiavo, Luigi. "The Temptation of Jesus: The Eschatological Battle and the New Ethic of the First Followers of Jesus in Q." *JSNT* 25.2 (2002) 141–64.

Segal, Arthur, and Michael Eisenberg. "Hercules in Galilee." *BAR* 37.6 (2011) 50–51.

Sloan, Robert B., Jr. *The Favorable Year of the Lord: A Study of Jubilary Theology in the Gospel of Luke*. Austin: Schola, 1997.

S'vyate Pys'mo. Staroho i Novoho Zavitu. London: Britans'ke y Zakordonne Bibliyne Tovarystvo [British and Foreign Bible Society], 1906.

Talbert, C. H. "The Myth of the Descending-Ascending Redeemer in Mediterranean Antiquity." *NTS* 22 (1976) 418–40.

Traina, Robert A. *Methodical Bible Study*. Grand Rapids: Zondervan, 1980.

van Kooten, George H. "Christianity in the Graeco-Roman World: Socio-Political, Philosophical, and Religious Interactions up to the Edict of Milan (CE 313)." In *The Routledge Companion to Early Christian Thought*, edited by D. Jeffrey Bingham. 3–37. New York: Routledge, 2010.

Vermes, Geza. *The Dead Sea Scrolls in English*. 3rd ed. Sheffield: Sheffield Academic, 1987.

Vetne, Riemar. "The Influence and Use of Daniel in the Synoptic Gospels." PhD diss., Andrews University, 2011. http://digitalcommons.andrews.edu/cgi/viewcontent.cgi?article=1159&context=dissertations.

Wall, Robert W, and Eugene E. Lemcio. *The New Testament as Canon: A Reader in Canonical Criticism*. Sheffield: Sheffield Academic, 1992.

Young, Frances. "Two Roots or a Tangled Mass?" In *The Myth of God Incarnate*, edited by John Hick, 87–121. London: SCM, 1977.

Zaleski, Carol, and Philip Zaleski. *The Fellowship: The Literary Lives of the Inklings; J. R. R. Tolkien, C. S. Lewis, Owen Barfield, Charles Williams*. New York: Farrar, Straus and Giroux, 2015.

CPSIA information can be obtained
at www.ICGtesting.com
Printed in the USA
BVHW091708171021
619128BV00009B/221